THE POWER OF THE PAUSE

Praise for Jillian Pransky's
THE POWER OF THE PAUSE

"Seamlessly blending her wisdom and insights from decades of teaching yoga and meditation, Jillian Pransky's *The Power of Pause* supports readers in accessing their internal 'reset buttons' to tap into an embodied experience of relaxation, through practices easily incorporated into daily life."

—**Sharon Salzberg,** *New York Times* bestselling author of *Real Happiness* and *Finding Your Way*

"Jillian's teachings are good medicine for our times. She offers accessible practices that can change the way we listen to ourselves and each other, essential tools at a time when we need them most. I so believe in the work she's doing and have experienced that medicine firsthand."

—**Dani Shapiro,** *New York Times* bestselling author of *Inheritance* and host of the podcast *Family Secrets*

"In this helpful and easy-to-read book, Jillian Pransky shows how Pausing is more than rest—it's an act of self-compassion. By calming the body, resetting the mind, and reconnecting with ourselves, we create the spaciousness needed for resilience, clarity, and genuine well-being."

—**Kristin Neff, PhD,** bestselling author of *Self-Compassion: The Proven Power of Being Kind to Yourself*

"*The Power of the Pause* offers a transformative yet accessible guide to finding calm amid chaos. . . . What sets this book apart is its practical approach—rather than demanding hours of formal meditation, Pransky provides realistic techniques that fit seamlessly into busy lives."

—**Shannon Watts,** *New York Times* bestselling author of *Fired Up: How to Turn Your Spark into a Flame and Come Alive at Any Age*

"Jillian Pransky bestows a timeless, precious gift—the preparation and conditions for listening. Pause allows us to hear the universe speak, from which the great truth emerges."

—**Lisa Miller, PhD,** *New York Times* bestselling author of *The Spiritual Child* and *The Awakened Brain*

"Jillian has created a masterful formula for finding inner help and strength in the most trying of moments that seem to arise unexpectedly. Following her simple practices enables one to recover and flourish unscathed in these tumultuous times."

—**Stephan Rechtschaffen, MD,** founder of Omega Institute and Blue Spirit

"*The Power of the Pause* is a tender guide to total presence. With each practice, we soften tension and open to clarity in order to discover the grace of real responsiveness. If you're seeking calm connection inwardly and outwardly, this book is for you."

—**Elena Brower,** bestselling author of *Practice You: A Journal* and *Hold Nothing*

"Jillian's timing is perfect! Her teachings in *The Power of the Pause* are just what the world needs right now."

—**Cyndi Lee,** bestselling author of *Yoga Body, Buddha Mind* and *May I Be Happy*

"Jillian Pransky shows us that Pausing isn't about stopping life—it's about finally being alive for it. *The Power of the Pause* . . . is your roadmap to steadiness, presence, and living fully awake."

—**Sah D'Simone,** bestselling author of *Spiritually Sassy* and *Spiritually, We*

"Informed by decades of teaching and studentship, Jillian shares the most essential practice for these times of constant distraction. Accessible and heartfelt, each chapter is a doorway that leads us deeper into trusting that not only can we Pause, but we are worthy of Pausing."

—**Tracee Stanley,** bestselling author of *Radiant Rest* and *The Luminous Self*

"Many of us are feeling the impact of being bombarded with a seemingly never-ending scroll of frightening information. . . . For those feeling the call to Pause, listen deeply, and live with a full heart, Jillian's work is a precious gift."

—**Micah Mortali,** author of *Rewilding* and founder of the Kripalu School of Mindful Outdoor Leadership

"Jillian poignantly emphasizes the profound habit of Pausing. She opens our hearts and minds to how this inner action can bring us home to ourselves."

—**Sarah Powers,** author of *Insight Yoga* and cofounder of the Insight Yoga Institute

"In the face of a threat or a surge of anger, Pausing first is actually a superpower. . . . Jillian Pransky gives us step-by-step guidance on how to practice doing just that. Don't wait until you're upset to start the practice."

—**Gail Parker, PhD, CIAYT,** author of *Restorative Yoga for Ethnic and Race-Based Stress and Trauma*

"An essential instruction manual for sanity for our times. This will become a staple for myself and for my teaching."

—**Christiane Wolf, MD, PhD,** author of *Mindfulness and Self-Compassion for Chronic Pain*

THE POWER OF THE PAUSE

90 SECONDS TO CALM, RESET, AND RECONNECT

JILLIAN PRANSKY

Dedicated to Pema Chödrön,
with immeasurable gratitude and love for the teachings.
And for your generosity, humor, and lightheartedness when sharing them.

ISBN 978-1-4549-5912-0
ISBN 978-1-4549-5913-7 (e-book)

Library of Congress Control Number: 2025943510

Sterling Ethos books may be purchased in bulk for business, educational, or promotional use. For more information,please contact your local bookseller or the Hachette Book Group's Special Markets department at special.markets@hbgusa.com.

Printed in Canada

2 4 6 8 10 9 7 5 3 1

unionsquareandco.com

"The Question" by Rosemerry Wahtola Trommer from *All the Honey* (Samara Press, 2023), reprinted courtesy of the author

Cover design by Patrick Sullivan
Cover art by Shutterstock.com/Kindlena
Interior design by Christine Heun

CONTENTS

WELCOME

I am excited for you to begin *The Power of the Pause.* In my thirty years of teaching people from all over the world, I can confirm that, on an unconscious level, most of us are living our lives on high alert. Our nervous system has been firing up our stress response so continuously that high alert now feels "normal." In this book, I teach how to dial down the stress response—to remain calm, centered, and compassionate, even during difficult conversations and experiences. *The Power of the Pause* offers a life-changing tool for creating calm, connection, and choice in our increasingly polarized and fractured world.

My work as a yoga therapist and meditation teacher led to my first book, *Deep Listening*, which appealed to yoga and meditation enthusiasts. But as my teaching expanded far beyond yoga, I realized we needed new tools to be able to access this same type of balance off the mat and out in the world. Practices to help us become more regulated, allowing us to hold and respond to the many complexities and challenges we face on a day-to-day basis.

This is essential because, in my classes and workshops, I have observed:

- We are used to living life as a series of reactions to whatever is happening around us, leaving us feeling stressed and overwhelmed much of the time.

- We live with so much tension in our bodies that it diminishes our health and well-being.
- We carry around emotional narratives and old stories that limit our ability to truly listen and to experience connection, growth, peace, and contentment.
- We get stuck in these old habits because of our survival wiring, and these habits keep our stories looping and our physiological tension building.
- We aren't taught how to slow down and be truly present or gentle—with ourselves, with each other, or with the world around us.

Today, our struggles are more heightened and widespread than I've seen in all my years of teaching. Many of us have been facing personal and community challenges for decades, and as a society, we are still dealing with all that the COVID pandemic brought to the world, as well as ongoing political and global turmoil. We are desperate to feel better in our bodies—physically and mentally—and in our relationships. In these times of societal, political, and ecological disarray, how can we find relief? How can we become more calm, centered, present, and conscious rather than shutting down or lashing out? How can we be more connected and compassionate together?

Pausing is the medicine for our times.

Many experts talk about the significance of pausing, but few share *how* to do it. And if they do, they do not include essential teachings about the body and nervous system that make pausing neurologically possible and therefore truly accessible.

The Power of the Pause weaves together the latest science on the stress response with real stories of how Pausing has changed people's lives and illustrates how it can change yours too. You will learn the Pause practice: a simple, short, repeatable mindfulness exercise that helps reduce stress and tension, cultivates somatic awareness and deep listening, and expands your capacity to choose the way you wish to participate with and respond to the present moment's conditions—both inside of you and around you. When you Pause, you have access to the parts of your brain that are responsible for big-picture thinking. You release hormones that foster your ability to connect with others and create relationships, help you feel more positive and optimistic, and generate new ideas and solutions.

In *The Power of the Pause*, I offer hands-on, accessible, effective teachings and practices for Pausing. These teachings have been the foundation of my work since 1998, but became a formal workshop in 2013 when I began teaching learning how to Pause annually at Kripalu Center for Holistic Living, Omega Institute, Esalen, and Mohonk Mountain House. Pausing is a practice that extends well beyond the yoga and mindfulness community. I have also presented this work to government officials in George Washington University's Center for Excellence in Public Leadership, as well as in keynotes and programs for corporations such as Genentech, La Roche, Condé Nast, Superfly, and Booz Allen Hamilton, and even to students at Wesleyan University, The New School, and Eugene Lang College of Liberal Arts.

In 2017, I began using the acronym **LAR-LAR** to help students remember how to practice Pausing and returning to a place of calm. How to release tension, create a sense of spaciousness, and feel a deeper connection in our bodies, minds, and hearts.

LAR-LAR quickly became the number one tool that supported students in integrating this practice into their day-to-day lives.

L—Land	A—Arrive	R—Relax
L—Listen	A—Attend	R—Respond (and Repeat)

LAR-LAR can be used by anyone, anywhere, anytime. You don't need to know how to do yoga or meditation to learn to Pause (although yoga and meditation have been shown to support this work greatly). You don't need special equipment or special clothes. You don't even need extra time in your day. There are plenty of ways to practice right in the middle of your daily routine. In fact, Pausing is *best* practiced right in the middle of your daily routine. And it can be done in just 90 seconds. Or even in just three breaths.

Pausing is the most immediate and reliable way to retrain our nervous system and self-regulate. Pausing is not a "holding" pattern. It's not a freeze or a time to "check out." Rather, pausing is a way we can ground ourselves while creating the space we need to better see, sense, and access what is happening in the present moment, inside and around us. This gives us the space we need to choose how we wish to participate in the present moment and respond to the current situation or circumstances. It is in the "magic" and ordinariness of self-regulation that we can bring ourselves into balance, showing up more in the present moment and taking care of ourselves and each other in a new way. Pausing can help us build the skills needed to nourish not only ourselves but also the relationships we value and the world we want to live in.

Imagine what it would be like to consciously slow down and reenter a challenging moment from a completely different perspective, whether you're in the heat of anger or feeling hurt, defensive, or ashamed.

Imagine what it would be like if in your moments of grief, illness, chronic pain, or anxiety, you were able to meet yourself with deep compassion and tenderness.

Imagine if you knew how to pause to savor a moment of joy, celebration, or beauty and really be present for these life-affirming experiences.

While reading *The Power of the Pause*, you may notice that some tools and instructions are repeated often. This is intentional, as learning often requires repetition.

The LAR-LAR practice for Pausing is a progressive six-step tool, with each step a foundation for the next. To help you best integrate the practices, I frequently refer to the previous steps as I move forward with instruction. Like building any new muscle, it's all about the reps.

Part One of this book will introduce the full practice of LAR-LAR. The first LAR (Land, Arrive, Relax) will help you set neurological conditions to Pause. The second LAR (Listen, Attend, Respond) will show how to use the Pause to become clearer, access your deeper wisdom and compassion, and expand your capacity for choice in the present moment.

In Part Two, you'll learn the incredible ways Pausing can transform our lives, relationships, and even the world.

In Part Three, I share extended practices to deepen your ability to Pause in all areas of your life, as well as essential information and techniques for how to practice Pausing when you are working with long-standing trauma or currently experiencing more acute high-level anxiety.

All of the LAR-LAR practices can be done standing or seated, or even laying down. Simply choose a position that you are most comfortable in. Please remember that, ultimately, you are learning to Pause on the spot, right in the middle of your day—and in the middle of any activity.

Lastly, to enhance your practice, I created audio recordings of all of the practices in *The Power of the Pause*, which are available to you for free through my website, jillianpransky.com.

To download these recordings, visit **https://jillianpransky.com /powerofthepause-practices** or access it through the QR Code below.

I am so happy to share this practice with you.

May these teachings benefit you and may the benefits ripple out into your relationships and the world around you.

PART ONE

PAUSING

In this section, we will learn how to use the LAR-LAR method to Pause. The first LAR (Land, Arrive, Relax) will help you reset your nervous system and create the conditions to Pause. The Second LAR (Listen, Attend, Respond) will show how to use the Pause to become clearer, access your deeper wisdom and compassion, and expand your capacity to choose your response in the present moment.

CHAPTER 1

Drop Your Shoulders

ALL MY LIFE, my mother told me to drop my shoulders.

"You look like a football player," she'd say.

"These are how my shoulders are!" I would say defensively. What I didn't realize at the time was that living in a house with my unpredictable and rage-filled father left me with the habit of hiking up my shoulders in protection. From plates being thrown around the kitchen to being kicked as a signal that it was time for me to leave the playground to fleeing to the neighbors' house after the police were called during one of his violent episodes, it often felt like I was living in a combat zone.

My dad controlled everything in our home, from the thermostat to the emotional climate. Fearing his anger and aggression, I learned to quickly appease him to keep the peace.

My mother was also often the target of my father's rage, and she, too, was looking for peace. In 1977, just nine years after the Beatles found meditation, my mother gave my father an ultimatum:

marriage counseling or Transcendental Meditation. A few weeks later, my mother enrolled my father, two brothers, and me in the TM Institute, where we spent several evenings in an incense-filled room in a New York City high-rise, receiving mantras from bearded men in white robes. At nine years old, simply traveling into Manhattan from our New Jersey home felt exotic, let alone stepping into this foreign culture. We were expected to meditate daily, on our own in the morning and again during family meditation time before dinner. Twice a day, my mother would set her kitchen timer for ten minutes, and I would chant my mantra silently, alone in my room. Eyes closed, sitting on my bed, back against the wall, I remember finding this ritual quite relaxing. It was a tiny break during which my parents were not fighting; no one was going to get in trouble for anything. There was no tension among us, even if it was only for ten minutes. It was a recess—a pause I so desperately needed. So, even though meditation was imposed, I found it a welcome refuge.

However, family meditation time didn't stick for more than a couple of months, if that long. My mother lost her enthusiasm for it, and my father quickly regained his throne. We were again subjected to his nightly explosions, and the tension level in the household returned to high alert.

It wasn't until my early twenties when I began practicing yoga and meditation regularly that I finally noticed how much tension I was holding in my shoulders. I also discovered my arms and fists were always activated and held in a tight sprinting position. Before that time, I did not recognize how armored up I was in the world; being in a ready-to-run position just felt natural.

There was something about the way I carried my body that felt normal—but also necessary. I wanted so badly to be included in my older brother's baseball game in the cul-de-sac we lived on, but not only was the bat too heavy for me, I was not *really* welcome in the boys club. As I grew up, I continually pushed myself to earn acknowledgment, inclusion, and appreciation in my male-dominated family. In second grade, I studied hard and was moved up a grade in math (into my brother's class, which, I recall, he was not too happy about). In fourth grade, I was one of only a handful of girls in our town's soccer league, and I became known for my slide tackle. I was tough enough to take down even the tallest boy on the other team. Starting in middle school, I was student council president every year through high school, as if it were my career.

As a go-getter from the get-go, I was born with lots of energy. I found myself continually absorbed in projects and goals and working toward accomplishments despite getting little support from the people who mattered to me most. From schoolwork and clubs to sports and friends, I was always actively participating. I became a person who could make things happen.

My enthusiastic nature continued as I grew into an adult. I graduated college with honors and accelerated through my early work years with accolades and promotions. And since working hard and "achieving" came easily to me, I never thought about it as something I developed in response to wanting to be seen, received, approved of, and *loved* by my dad. I wanted this even more than I wanted to protect myself from him (an awareness that came much later).

Only when I was successful by my father's standards and in ways he deemed valid—slide-tackling a boy during a soccer game, being elected class president, getting a raise at work—would he acknowledge me. And then, it was only to others—"My daughter is a tough soccer player!"—rather than to me directly. Of course, I loved it when I overheard him say these things, yet at the same time, it made me angry that he couldn't say them directly to me.

I did receive occasional reprieves from my father's aggression when he was convalescing. He suffered several major heart attacks, kidney failure, a variety of cancers, and was even in a serious coma after driving his sports car under a truck. Every two years or so, he went from throne to hospital bed with one of these many life-threatening conditions. Throughout my childhood and late into my teens, I was either hiding from him, appeasing him, or suffering his wrath while oscillating between wishing he was no longer on the planet and begging God for his survival.

My dad did not only rule my shoulders; he ruled my mind and behavior. So much of what I thought about, and how I acted and reacted in the world, was dictated by the wounds I had collected within this relationship, both physically and emotionally. Eventually I came to understand that under my defending shoulders, I harbored fear and anxiety. And under my fear and anxiety was a deep longing for approval, validation, safety, and love.

Before learning that accessing approval, validation, safety, and love was an inside job, they were big topics of exploration for me, as I worked hard to perform for teachers, coaches, bosses, and authority figures of all kinds. I also kept myself "productive" all the time. Even my downtime was about accomplishing, whether in the gym or cleaning my apartment. I always had to be working toward something.

For example, at twenty-three years old, having run my first 5-mile race only five months before, my boss gave me a ticket to run in the 26.2-mile New York City Marathon. Wanting to impress him and thinking this was just another mind-over-matter opportunity, I took the spot and ran. To say I was utterly unprepared for this type of physical feat is an understatement, and my push to perform and achieve took its toll. I finished the race, but I bottomed out for almost a year with chronic fatigue, a variety of viruses, and a deep pull to find relief. Then I wandered into a yoga class in a studio I passed every day on the way to work.

The stark, vast room had windows flanking one side with sheer white curtains hanging against the white walls. I remember the thick smell of incense was nag champa, the same that had been burning when I went to the meditation school with my family years before. I immediately felt at ease. At the end of the two-hour class, after pushing through challenging yoga poses and sitting still in meditation, we were invited to lie on our backs on the floor and rest. Completely. Fully. Like there was nothing to do ever again. Deep rest in yoga is called Corpse Pose, and I instantly understood why.

As I lay on the ground, allowing the earth to hold me, I felt as if I could stop holding everything inside me so tightly. The support of the ground underneath me allowed me to soften all my muscles. There became room for my breath to expand, which opened up a feeling of space in my body, heart, and mind. Through this space, emotions just started to flow: a torrent of anger, sadness, and shame that had felt stuck in my body for a lifetime.

This was obviously not "relaxing" in the traditional sense, yet the release of historic tension was profoundly healing. I felt more openness in my body and mind than I had ever felt before. While this experience was indescribably soothing, the feeling of my "armor" dropping away was unfamiliar, and the sense of vulnerability that took its place scared me a little. As I lay on my spongy blue yoga mat, what emerged from this release was immense relief as well as an awareness of an intense grief that I'd been carrying around for a very long time. I mourned how I "wanted" things to be and cried in relief that I could finally *feel* it all and no longer *unconsciously* harbor it in my body.

It felt like I was releasing a lifetime of stress and tension. As I rested and softened, I could feel the ground under my body—supporting me—for the first time ever.

I Landed.

My shoulders dropped. This was the relief and the ease that I had been seeking for so long.

In my go-getter way, I returned to yoga class seven days a week for three years and soon signed up for teacher training.

Studying yoga and meditation deeply was life-changing for me—physically, mentally, and emotionally—and this led me to want to share what I had discovered with others. After a decade in publishing, I left my longtime job to teach yoga and meditation.

In 1995, there were not a lot of yoga teachers in the New York City area—or anywhere, for that matter. Yoga studios were few and far between; they had yet to proliferate in the culture. As a result, the handful of us who were certified instructors were regularly invited to lead "yoga events" wherever they were offered, whether at corporations or the local YMCA.

Three years later, as a relatively new teacher, I received an incredible invitation: Omega Institute for Holistic Studies in Rhinebeck, New York, asked me to lead the yoga program during a retreat taught by Buddhist Master and renowned author Pema Chödrön.

Starting in the late 1990s, Pema Chödrön became known as one of the primary teachers who popularized Tibetan-Buddhist teachings and practices of mindfulness for the layperson and seasoned meditator alike. This was my first exposure to her, and in order to craft yoga classes that would resonate with and enrich her students' experience, I read her book, *When Things Fall Apart*. Brilliant, funny, and compassionate, she had me from page one.

Though I was first introduced to the practice of pausing by Yoga Master Erich Schiffmann, Pema taught me a more "formal" technique. She used a three-breath pause as a tool to help students stop and open into the present moment more fully and freshly. At that time it was relatively simple. Stop for three breaths; be with each breath as fully as possible, as it is happening; then expand your awareness (through hearing or seeing) into the space around you.

In the yoga classes that I taught at her retreats, I would incorporate how to pause physically, in our bodies. In yoga poses, through guided instruction, I would invite students to feel their bodies on the ground. Here. Now. I asked them to return to their bodies and feel the support that is *always* underneath them—*always underneath us all.*

Students shared how, as they Landed in their bodies, breathed more deeply, and began to relax, a true Pause became more accessible. One after another, they would describe how their feelings of tension and anxiety started to shift and lessen. They would say that this was the first time they could feel the ground holding them, the first time they could truly let themselves feel supported, receive their breath more fully, and *safely* experience what was happening inside and outside their bodies. And I could see it happening to them.

This feedback from students confirmed what I had experienced in my own practice as I worked through my own tension and anxiety: Pausing must begin in the body. It's a physical, somatic practice. I discovered that Pausing not only sets the conditions for opening the mind and allowing for *choice* over *reaction*, but it also forms the foundation for true relaxation—an essential tool for self-regulation.

This understanding was crucial as I worked through my anxiety. Right around this time, my beloved thirty-four-year-old sister-in-law passed away after a three-year fight with cancer. I was only a few years younger than her, and this was the first time in my life that I had to truly confront mortality—hers and my own. This was hard for me, as it would be for anyone, but I saw myself as a strong person, so I pulled myself together and drove down to Maryland from New Jersey to help my brother clean out her closet. As my husband and I were driving home, my arms went numb and I started to shiver. I felt dizzy and short of breath. I was sure I was having a heart attack, and I ended up in the Emergency Room. It turned out to be my first panic attack, and it felt like an earthquake shaking the foundations of my life. After that initial attack, I went through months of acute anxiety. Things I used to do regularly, without ever thinking twice—ride the subway, fly in a plane, drive on the highway—now seemed threatening. I had this feeling that I was constantly running away from danger. I could feel my arms tense up again, locked in that familiar sprinting position.

I recall a specific day when I had to go to work but could not even leave our apartment. I became terrified about what was happening to me, fearful that I might never get my life back. It was at this moment that things shifted. I remembered there was a tool—my yoga and meditation practice. I remembered I had something to lean on.

Before my bout with anxiety and panic, my daily yoga practice consisted of rolling out my yoga mat. But I felt too shaky and fragile to do my "usual" routine. Then I realized I could practice getting grounded with the same tools anywhere, anytime. No mat necessary.

In the small kitchen of our fourth-floor walk-up in Hoboken, New Jersey, I sat at the table and brought my attention to my seat on my chair. I felt my feet on the ground. I let my weight drain down into my seat, legs, and feet. I placed my hands on my belly. Even though I was tense, simultaneously tired and wired, I was able to focus on the support of my chair and the ground below me and then my breath moving underneath my hands. Arriving on my breath, I calmed and grew more present. I felt like I could actually rest again for the first time in months—and this began the process of unwinding deep tension I'd been holding. This began my practice of Pausing on the spot, off my mat, throughout my day, often.

From that point on, I continued to dedicate myself to learning how to adapt my practices to help me return to feelings of groundedness and presence. So I could Pause and step back into the moment with more calm, clarity, and resources.

Once I was able to feel grounded more often, I could explore the roots of my panic attacks and anxiety. I realized that my sister-in-law's death had triggered them, but I also recognized that I was still harboring a lifetime of unresolved feelings toward my dad stored in my body.

All of our experiences, emotions, and thoughts can be stored in our bodies. We cannot process them as they arise for many reasons—we may not be safe enough to do so or we may not yet know how to. And the harder these emotions are for us to meet in real time, the deeper they get stored within us.

I now know that my tension was the stress response finding a home in my body. I've learned that by changing my relationship with that tension, I was able to shift my levels of anxiety.

As my practice became more integrated into my daily life, I learned that when I was grounded, I could purposely drop my shoulders, unfurl my fists, and be more present and compassionate with myself and the current conditions of my life, whatever they happened to be.

For the next twenty-five years, I was invited back to Omega to teach yoga during Pema Chödrön's retreats, sometimes twice a year. These ongoing opportunities to receive her teachings—and immediately weave them into my classes—deepened my understanding of her work and Buddhist meditation principles. I gained insight into how we react to others, ourselves, and the world through the lens of deep-seated, often historical, tensions, feelings, and emotions that we carry in our bodies over a lifetime. How we perceive danger and safety shapes the lens through which we see and hear the world. From this lens, our behavior emerges—our stories, habits, and reactions.

I learned how, once we begin to befriend and care for the parts of ourselves that we have habitually ignored or rejected, we are able to listen deeply and show up in our lives more fully and compassionately.

What I have come to understand through Pema's work, my own practice, and teaching has been validated by groundbreaking research from leading scientists, doctors, and neurologists. Research shows that we are better able to Pause when we create certain somatic conditions, and how the Pause itself, in turn, creates physiological benefits, including reducing our stress response, lowering heart rate, optimizing respiratory function, enhancing digestion, and so many more aspects of our physical health and well-being. More importantly, the impact Pausing has on our neurological well-being can create changes in how we respond by expanding our capacity for learning, curiosity, bonding, and the ability to be in more mindful and compassionate relationships.

After decades of teaching the Pause in classes, workshops, and retreats, one thing I know for certain is that most people can't simply "pause" on command—especially when they're stressed, which is when they need it the most. Just telling someone to Pause is the same thing as telling someone to relax when they are all wound up. How do you feel when a loved one tells you to "just relax"? If you are anything like me, you probably feel even more uptight.

I remember Richard, one of my workshop students, sharing in our closing circle, "We all have heard about the pause. Everybody says just take a breath, count to ten. And that's easy to say. And I think I, for one, know I've counted to ten and ended up being angrier at the end of ten."

This experience makes sense. Our brains are designed NOT to pause when we are feeling threatened, defensive, scared, or anxious. This is when our brains instantly shift into autopilot mode to do the fastest thing we can to survive. In other words, we rely on our unconscious reactions, rather than our mindful responses, to keep us safe.

We may not be able to Pause automatically. But we can learn to Pause through practice so that the skill is available to us when we need it most. Whether it's in the middle of a heated conversation with our partner or the moment before we hit Send on that email . . . whether it's soothing ourselves in the face of grief or responding to someone whose belief system is entirely counter to our own, Pausing can give us the space we need to act in a way that we can feel good about rather than potentially regret.

My confidence in the benefits and effectiveness of Pausing has grown with each year of teaching. I've seen that when we turn our attention to the way we *are* supported by what is under our body—whether it's the ground, a chair, a couch, the earth—we allow our bodies to settle more fully, creating the foundation needed to bring ourselves into a state of greater ease. When we feel held, we can begin to release our hunched shoulders so that more breath can flow through us. As our posture relaxes and opens, our breath flows more fully and deeply, sending a message to our brain that we can begin to downshift from stress toward relaxation. This slowing down, even for a few moments, allows us to Pause more and create a greater sense of space and ease in our bodies and minds.

At the end of our workshop, Richard said, "You taught me how to do this. You gave me a formula. I am not a person who feels my body very much, and I really don't particularly like stretching or yoga. So, learning to land in my body and feel grounded really made all the difference. But it's not just Land, Arrive, Relax. It's a way of being. I can choose to do this over and over again. I can calm myself all day long."

Richard's experience of relief, ease, and the empowerment to repeat the practice is one I hear all the time. The thousands of teachers and therapists I have trained also report that they have experienced enormous, life-changing shifts from this simple practice.

Pausing allows us to slow down, calm ourselves, clear our minds, and choose to respond rather than react from a habitual pattern or behavior that we've seasoned all our lives through our conditioning, our relationships with others and the world, and our nervous system. It allows us to take "redos" after regretful actions. Pausing can also help us take less regrettable actions in the first place and instead respond more purposefully, mindfully, and compassionately.

Pausing has helped me in every area of my life, from conflicts with family and parenting challenges to prioritizing downtime and increasing productivity at work. It has guided me through grief and allowed me to be more present for others during their struggles. I've also learned to stay grounded in my body and breath and to create the boundaries I need to care for myself with compassion. Over time, my ability to Pause with my dad allowed us to find a new way of relating to each other. And I've learned to drop my shoulders—something I continue to do *repeatedly*, as this is, after all, a lifelong practice.

CHAPTER 2

At the Table

It was the Friday night after Thanksgiving. My mother was visiting us from Florida, and she, my daughter Willow, and I were having a meandering conversation around the table after dinner. We wandered into hot topics (social, political, and cultural news)—an eighty-two-year-old, twenty-year-old, and fifty-five-year-old who didn't always see eye to eye. It was getting late, and I was trying to savor our time together, although I was a little too full and overtired.

Then Willow, seemingly out of the blue, made what I thought was a mean comment to my mom that shot me straight up in my seat. I don't even remember specifically what she said, only that in an instant, my whole head was on fire, and I glared at her in disbelief.

My mother didn't seem offended—or perhaps she simply wanted to avoid stirring up conflict. But Willow and I were already in a death-stare battle.

I launched at Willow with some punitive words. She needed to understand that her comment to my mother, her grandmother, was out of line. What could have been a teaching moment quickly escalated into a sharp scolding. In response, Willow doubled down, saying something that only fueled my fire.

Not wanting to ruin Thanksgiving, I abruptly left the table, dumped my dishes in the sink, slammed a kitchen cabinet closed, and stormed upstairs to sequester myself in my bathroom.

Flipped My Lid

Basically, at the table, I lost my mind—and not just metaphorically. Neuropsychologist Dan Siegel, executive director of the Mindsight Institute and founding co-director of the Mindful Awareness Research Center at UCLA, explains that when we are feeling stressed—which can include feeling threatened, defensive, scared, anxious, attacked, or even insulted—our prefrontal cortex, the front lobe of our brain, goes offline. Our brains and bodies go on autopilot mode to do the fastest, most habitual thing we can do to survive. Often, before we can even create a story from or assign meaning to our stress, we have everything we need to fight or flee.

Let me emphasize that our physiological reactions in the face of stress are automatic and largely unconscious. They happen whether we want them to or not: Our heart and breathing rates increase. Our muscles tense. These physical reactions are called somatic experiences; in other words, they are *experienced in the body*.

I will talk a lot about the stress response and its role in our ability to Pause in Part Two, but for now, it's key to know that it happens *instantly and automatically*. This emotional response is what people are referring to when they say "triggered."

Our *stress response* gets "triggered."

In the Bathroom

While in the bathroom, taking refuge from my family, my heart was racing. My jaw was clenched, my shoulders were hunched up to my ears, my fists were balled up tight. Barely able to put thoughts together, I was overwhelmed with anger from Willow's disrespect and seeming lack of remorse when I suddenly realized I had *left* the table.

"Fuck, fuck, fuck . . ." I said out loud, dread sinking in.

Here's some backstory: Just three days earlier, my agent sent my book proposal to publishers, and one of the working titles was *Stay at the Table.*

"Dammit . . . I'm writing a book about how to stay at the table. I have to go back."

Easier said than done, considering the state I was in.

When we are stressed, we are designed not to let our guard down until we believe there is no more immediate danger. This instinct makes sense. If the brain perceives danger—say, if a lion is chasing us—it's essential not to take time to pause and consider our options. Rather, our job is to just get out of there alive. Quickly. In other words, we rely on our automatic, habitual reactions to "survive" rather than our mindful responses.

While this is brilliant and a fundamentally necessary design when we are truly in physical danger, there is a cost. The stress response also turns off the part of the brain responsible for big-picture thinking, making decisions, expansive awareness, and connections. And, as you might agree, while we may not be running from lions regularly, there is no shortage of perceived daily "dangers" . . . whether it is a driver cutting us off, monthly bills, the news, climate change, world events, or even a fight with our family at the kitchen table.

On top of this, everyone's stress is personal. For one person, jumping on an airplane is a delight and for another it's an absolute terror. We are all triggered by experiences in our lives as we see them through our own lens—our conditioning that includes our upbringing, our historic wounds, and even what happened yesterday.

We don't need to *judge* what pushes our own buttons or anyone else's buttons. The truth is, the specific comment that Willow made doesn't matter. What matters is that something made me shut down, and I fled.

We all have ideas about what is right or wrong. We all have opinions about whether someone is justified in losing their cool, ending their marriage, disciplining their kids, saying something cutting or hurtful, or storming out of a room. And these reactions impact all of our interactions. So a central question we will answer in *The Power of the Pause* is how we can open up to our own stuff and each other's stuff—not to call it right or wrong, or appropriate or inappropriate—but rather to understand that we are all having reactions to our own discomfort all the time.

To open up, we must purposely shut off our *autopilot* and interrupt our stress response. We initiate steps to quell the physical reactions that have taken hold in our body, which will simultaneously begin to calm the mind.

What *Was Actually* Happening in the Bathroom?

First off, when I slammed the door to my bathroom (my beloved refuge), I was more than stressed. I was furious, and it felt totally justified. Jaw clenched, shoulders hunched, fists tight—I held my breath to contain the familiar anger exploding inside me.

Despite my not *wanting* to go back downstairs, after years of practicing Pausing, I knew it was exactly what I needed. But even so, I started my Pause practice begrudgingly.

Just three breaths into it, it did what it always does. It began to shift my perspective. As my body relaxed, I could feel my rising desire for repair and reconnection.

I *wanted* the resources to go back to the table clearer, more present, and more regulated, to work out our differences or at least communicate from a less reactive place.

The amazing thing is, even with my initial resistance, 90 seconds later, I entered a completely different state. And, just minutes after my dramatic exit, I was back at the table.

Introducing LAR-LAR

Once I remembered that my Pause practice was actually there, waiting for me, I began to go through the six steps of **LAR-LAR**, the acronym that has helped my students remember the order of how to support themselves and shift their nervous system. Here is the short version:

Step #1. I took a breath to **LAND**. To feel grounded.
Step #2. I took another breath to **ARRIVE**. As I followed my breath into my body, my mind arrived with it, into the present moment.
Step #3. I took another breath to **RELAX**, on purpose, to feel more at ease in my body.

These first three steps interrupt the stress response and initiate the state of Pausing.

Step #4. I allowed myself to **LISTEN**. To perceive more clearly what was actually happening in the present moment, the feelings under my anger.
Step #5. I **ATTENDED** to myself, meeting and caring for all the feelings, thoughts, and experiences that arose in my body and mind.
Step #6. Feeling clearer, calmer, and more cared for, I was ready to **RESPOND** with greater intention and compassion to the situation at hand. I wanted to go back to the table.

These final three steps create the space to fully embrace the present moment and consciously choose how to engage with it.

In just moments, I was changed. This practice not only allowed me to go back downstairs, but also transformed how I could respond to Willow when I returned to the table. I was now able to calmly participate in the conversation, listen, and rationally choose my words and actions. This changed everything.

There's a part of me that wonders whether someone would read that list of LAR-LAR steps and think, *oh, that's a lot* . . . or roll their eyes and think, *there is no way some silly acronym is going to help my relationship with my kids, my partner, my parents, my neighbor, my boss.*

But for years my students have felt this silly acronym do exactly that. And now you can, too. Because every time you LAR-LAR, you'll increase your ability to regulate your nervous system as well as *understand yourself and those around you*, allowing the possibility for more ease and peace on the planet, rather than more aggression.

Imagine Having the Space to Choose

What if we could Pause before saying that hurtful comment in a fight? Before raising our voice to our child, or sending an email we'll regret? What if we could hold back from flipping off that driver, slamming the cabinet, or devouring that whole sheet of brownies?

Now, imagine Pausing in even more intense situations, such as when we're judged unfairly for our beliefs, our skin color, or our life choices. Imagine finding the clarity to respond with calm and strength.

What if, in moments of anger, hurt, or shame, we could slow down, shift our perspective, and enter the moment with a clear mind?

Picture being able to meet ourselves with compassion during grief, illness, or anxiety, and soothe ourselves enough to be fully present for those we care about.

And what if, in moments of joy, ease, or celebration, we could Pause long enough to truly savor them—so we don't miss out on the richness of life happening right in front of us?

Pausing gives us the space to be fully present in our lives. It reminds us that *this* matters—life matters. We matter. This moment is worth experiencing, and it's worth choosing how we want to show up, and how we want to participate and respond. Pausing sets the conditions we need in our body and mind to choose our response.

As philosopher and Holocaust survivor Viktor Frankl, author of *Man's Search for Meaning*, brilliantly proposed, "Between stimulus and response, there is a space. In that space is our power to choose our response. In our response lies our growth and our freedom."

I don't remember the first time I discovered this quote, but I know it stopped me in my tracks. For the next two decades, I devoted myself to exploring what it means to be in *that* space.

Pausing is how we create this space, and LAR-LAR is how we Pause.

A Word About Pausing

Pausing isn't simply "just stopping." It's an intentional, conscious break we take. This distinction matters because, as I mentioned, the mind goes offline when we are stressed. And this raises a central question: If our mind is not "available" to Pause, how do we do it?

Because we are working with ancient neurological wiring that keeps us constantly on alert and triggering our stress response, in order to Pause, we need to *consciously* interrupt this antiquated system—often.

It is also important to understand that we can't do it on command. Just telling someone to Pause is the same thing as telling someone to *relax* when they are all wound up. If my mom had told me to relax or Pause while I was at the table in that conversation, I would have surely gotten more riled up.

Rather than "thinking about Pausing," we must begin this process in the body. Pausing is a *somatic* practice, and we can train ourselves to do this through LAR-LAR. We start with feeling supported in our body to expand our breath, release excess tension, and self-regulate. When the body is more grounded and calm, we can begin to access clearer thinking and a more mindful presence.

The more we can self-regulate, the more flexible our nervous system is for the most appropriate response, and the more access we have to a wider array of conscious choices—as well as our wisdom and compassion.

Just to emphasize, we're not naturally designed to Pause when we're stressed—it's part of our evolutionary wiring, not something personal. While Pausing might feel out of reach for many of us, it's mostly because we've never really trained ourselves to do it. We can learn, even if it doesn't happen automatically yet.

If we train in Pausing regularly, we can create new habits to replace our old habitual reactions. It expands our ability to self-regulate and recondition our nervous system, enabling us to access the skill of Pausing more often and when we need it most.

Pausing can help re-wire our nervous system to handle stressors more effectively. It won't magically make them disappear, but it allows us to develop a new relationship with them—so we can navigate through challenges in a healthier way.

CHAPTER 3

Land

A FEW YEARS ago, after Hurricane Ian, I visited my mom in southwest Florida. The storm had wreaked havoc in her area: Boats were scattered in the street, cars were submerged in water, couches and beds were strewn across lawns, and roofs had landed in driveways.

Wildlife were not where they should be, either: Sea turtles sought refuge in pools, alligators wandered through shopping center parking lots, and pythons nestled inside garages for shelter.

Although not typically aggressive killers, pythons are known for their painful bite and, when threatened, may squeeze their prey to death. And, they're terrifyingly huge—like the fifteen-footer that roamed the neighborhood after the storm. I'd always been scared of the small, nonvenomous snakes that slithered around my mom's property, so when I saw the python's dramatic glamour shots on TV and social media, I was determined not to run into it.

On this morning, the mail carrier accidentally delivered a neighbor's package to my mom's house. I called the neighbor to ask when would be a good time for me to drop it off, and she said they'd be home in a couple of hours. After lunch, I headed over. As I approached their plastic pink flamingos marking the shortcut through our yards, I heard a lot of rustling in the bushes. Before consciously thinking *python*, I found myself sprinting back to my mom's.

When I was safe in the kitchen, out of breath and still shaken, the phone rang. It was the neighbor calling to say her husband had just finished up trimming the bushes in the backyard and he would be able to come and pick up the package.

"Husband in the bushes!" I laughed to myself and took a deep breath.

Despite the humor of mistaking her husband for a python, my body was still trembling.

Reptilian Brain and the Stress Response

The human brain has evolved, over millions of years, in three basic stages: the reptilian brain (or brain stem), the mammalian brain (or limbic system), and the primate brain (or cortex).

The reptilian brain is the oldest part of the brain and was the first to develop in all creatures on the planet. It is called the reptilian brain because it is the same part found in reptiles and has remained largely unchanged throughout evolution. This means our reptilian brain is essentially the same as that of our ancient ancestors.

The reptilian brain is responsible for all of our most basic, automatic functions—those we don't have to think about and that keep us alive even while we are sleeping, such as respiration and heart rate. It also serves as our first line of defense when we are in danger, with the sole function of ensuring our survival.

This part of the brain includes the amygdala, which is central to our most primal emotions, particularly fear—commonly referred to as our *fear circuitry*. It processes sensory information and uses that input to learn what's dangerous. If we encounter something similar in the future, our amygdala will generate a feeling of fear based on previous experiences.

From an evolutionary perspective, fear is crucial for our survival. It triggers our stress response—the ability to protect ourselves through a "fight, flight, freeze" reaction. The stress response initiates in the precise moment we perceive—see, smell, touch, or sense—danger, even before we can interpret the threat. This is why the reptilian brain is the fastest responder of the three parts of the brain. In less than one-twentieth of a second, less than the time between two heartbeats, it initiates biochemical, neurological, and physiological reactions to help us stay alive. Immediately, we release a cascade of hormones (chemical messengers) needed to respond to danger: cortisol, adrenaline, and epinephrine.

Survival mode needs to turn on automatically; we don't have time to consciously ponder and make decisions about how to stay alive—our brain compels us to survive.

This was the case for me when I thought I heard a python. My dutiful amygdala was on the lookout for the at-large python. The moment I heard the rustling noises in the bushes, my brain, already primed for survival, was quick to assume the worst. Whether the rustle was in fact a python or simply a husband trimming the bushes was of no concern to my amygdala. If a rustle *could be* a python, that would be enough for my fear circuitry to kick in.

Once our brain detects a potential threat, it shifts our body and mind into survival mode, preparing us to run from—or, in extreme cases, fight—a perceived danger, even if it isn't actually there.

Don't Stop to Think About Tomorrow

When we shift into the stress response, our bodies' priorities shift, too. Systems meant for long-term survival, like digestion and immunity, temporarily shut down. The future doesn't matter when facing a python—only the present moment does. Our bodies focus solely on what makes us faster, stronger, and able to react instantly: Our breath quickens, our heart rate spikes, and our muscles tighten, giving us the immediate strength and energy we need to face the threat. The hormone surge and muscle tension keep us from resting, ensuring that we stay alert and ready to move.

Besides sacrificing our systems of homeostasis, the amazing autopilot process of the stress response causes us to "flip our lids," as Dr. Dan Siegel describes. The prefrontal cortex, responsible for bigger-picture thinking and higher-order reasoning, goes offline, and we lose access to our creative problem-solving abilities. We actually *can't* stop to think about tomorrow.

Over our lifetime, we are designed to continually acquire stories about potential dangers—about pythons and many other things that we may never encounter—so our brain can get better at recognizing danger. This way, we get even better at initiating our autopilot successfully, again and again.

That day in Florida, my brain reacted instantly in order to survive. It never occurred to me to stop and wonder whether it really *was* a python in the bushes. My sense of hearing called up a memory of "snake," and I bolted. I wasn't curious about the python at all. I didn't have the time or space to consider any of the wide array of creatures—or husbands—that could have made a rustle in the bushes.

We usually regard stress as something that happens only in our mind, but really, our whole body gets hijacked by the experience and the energy of not feeling safe. I was exposed to something that *might* be a threat, and my brain instantly commanded: Run!

What Are You Afraid Of?

Like the oldest animals on the planet, we mobilize in the face of threat. However, unlike those ancient creatures, we are not only afraid of the "real" things out in the world—lions, tigers, and pythons—but we also become anxious about our internal experiences: our thoughts, emotions, and physical sensations. We ruminate on personal stories, narratives we have internalized, and those inherited from our families and even our ancestors.

This phenomenon is another function of our fear circuitry. It is an adaptive response, but over time, it can leave us feeling perpetually unsafe. While our fear circuitry is evolutionarily wired to initiate our defense mode in response to environmental threats, we engage this same system for all sources of stress, whether they're coming from outside of us or from inside of us. We wind up engaging our survival response in the face of anything that makes us feel "not okay."

For many of us, our nervous system has been triggering our stress response from these internal experiences so continuously that high alert now feels "normal."

Remember, this repeated activation of our stress response is an innate function of our survival wiring, but it can often lead to chronic stress and the loss of our ability to respond appropriately to danger and safety. This loss of flexibility in our nervous system—the ability to flow back and forth between stress and safety—is often referred to as "dysregulation," or the inability to regulate ourselves.

Soothing the Reptilian Brain

To interrupt our ancient fear circuitry, we need to learn how to self-regulate and soothe the reptilian brain. In other words, after our stress response is activated and the threat has passed—and we are still alive—our body needs to shift back into a resting state, known as the "relaxation response."

Simply put, the relaxation response (also known as "rest and digest mode") is the opposite of our body's stress response—the "off switch" to our fight-or-flight mode—which *should* automatically activate when we feel safe.

The relaxation response moves us from the state of surviving back toward thriving. Our blood pressure and heart rate lower, breathing slows, muscles relax, blood sugar regulates, and blood flows to our digestive organs. All the organs and systems for long-term health and healing receive a return of blood flow and optimization. Additionally, it quiets the fear center and reactivates the prefrontal cortex. This allows us to expand our awareness and have access to bigger-picture thinking and a wider range of options when making decisions.

Our relaxation response *should* kick in automatically when we are not in acute stress, but often it doesn't. Most of us live our lives as if we are continually *on the run*, and the body's relaxation response doesn't have time to activate before our next stressful moment occurs. The hormone dump and mobilizing activities of the stress response keep us from resting. We tend to walk around all day long and even go to bed at night without giving our full weight to the support that *is* underneath us—whether it's a chair, couch, bed, floor, ground, or the earth itself. And, when we feel ungrounded, we may not only feel easily thrown off balance, but also anxious and vulnerable. We end up working harder to protect ourselves, amplifying our efforts to "stay safe and avoid danger." This is not a personality or character flaw; it's simply a brain on stress.

Feeling unsupported sends messages to the nervous system that we are not safe. Feeling ungrounded often exaggerates a sense of separateness, disconnection, isolation, and loneliness. We wonder who will catch us, who is in our corner, who has our back. An antidote to feeling ungrounded is to consciously return to our connection to physical support—the surfaces and structures that literally have our backs, and our feet, and our legs . . .

To initiate the relaxation response, we need to consciously communicate safety to the reptilian brain, which is a process that begins in and through the body. We need to create conditions to believe it is indeed safe to rest, sending messages of safety regardless of what's happening around us. When we bring our attention to what is underneath us and allow ourselves to be supported, everything changes.

What's amazing is that initiating the relaxation response can happen more quickly and simply than you might imagine. This is what LAR-LAR offers and why it always begins with Landing.

Landing is the moment you truly feel that there is support under your body, and you allow yourself to rest on it: to be held up *by* that support, rather than *holding yourself up*.

When we are stressed, all the muscles in our body tense, perpetuating the fight-or-flight mode. We cannot begin to relax if our body is tensed for motion in this way. That's why we begin learning how to Pause by focusing on the body and its muscles, with the psoas being a key player in this physical process.

A Short (Psoas) Story

When I teach Landing, I always start by talking about the psoas. I know you didn't pick up this book for an anatomy lesson. But I'm going to ask you to trust me here, because knowing a bit about the body and the psoas muscle in particular can shift how we approach challenging situations.

For starters, psoas is pronounced *so-as*. We have two of them, one on either side of the body—but its name is said and written the same, whether singular or plural. For this conversation, I'll refer to it singularly.

The psoas is the only muscle in the body that connects our legs to our torso and plays a primary role in our ability to walk, run, stand, and balance. It is the psoas that initiates dynamic defensive movements like kicking, punching, or running for our life. We cannot begin to relax into a moment of Pause if our body is contracted into a sprinting posture or a fighting stance.

Most importantly, the psoas is directly linked to the reptilian brain, which governs our basic survival instincts. It is in direct, continual communication with our nervous system and fear circuitry. The psoas muscle is so finely tuned to our environment that "psoas experts" (there are such things) consider it an "organ of perception."

This means that when we perceive danger, even if we don't know exactly what we need protection from, in that one-twentieth of a second I mentioned earlier, our psoas muscle shortens and activates—giving us the ability to fight or flee instantly. The psoas can also immediately curl us into a ball to "play dead" (freeze). This "curling" action protects all our vital organs and tamps down their functionality. This response is by design; when we are hiding and trying to play dead, we don't want a predator hearing our breathing. However, while life-saving, this shortening simultaneously compromises the very organs it's protecting.

It is also worth taking a moment to better understand the location of the psoas. Running from the mid-spine and attaching to the upper inner thigh bone, the psoas is like a hammock, strung from the inner thigh and lying behind all the organs of the pelvis and abdomen up to where the diaphragm meets the spine.

A muscle so close to our diaphragm—our breathing center—is going to affect not only our breathing but all the organs nearby. The psoas is so intertwined with all the organs in the torso that, when contracted, it acts almost like too-tight plastic wrap, minimizing their ability to function optimally. It restricts diaphragmatic movement and lung expansion, interrupts optimal digestive function, diminishes flow and function around all the pelvic and abdominal organs, and more. Lastly, when contracted, it also pulls on the spine, creates misalignments, and is at the root of much of our back and hip pain.

While tight shoulders or sore feet may benefit from a good stretch, the psoas is more complex. As a servant of our survival instinct, the psoas can only be released from its contracted state if we feel safe. In other words, the psoas will stay contracted unless it gets the message: It's safe to rest.

When tense and restricted—ready to run—a contracted psoas also prevents us from fully Landing and resting on the ground. It prevents us from feeling ourselves on the earth—held up by the support under our bodies—which further activates our stress response.

In contrast, a more supple, responsive psoas is the key to our ability to sense our body on the ground and, in turn, support this shift into relaxation. Hence, when we are in a state of calm, we describe it as feeling grounded.

Its direct and intimate relationship to our nervous system makes the psoas a perfect entry point for lowering our stress and anxiety in the body. While there are many practices in yoga and techniques in physical therapy to help release tension in the psoas, we can also do this in our daily life simply by learning to let our bodies be held up by support. When we consciously sense the support under our body, literally allowing our body weight to release and rest on the ground—or whatever is underneath us—it sends a powerful message to the nervous system that we are safe and free from danger, and then we can relax more.

Therefore, sensing support and then safety helps us settle into the Pause.

Meghan's Story

Meghan first contacted me in response to a blog post I had written about my own experience of anxiety. She believed she was falling apart and was searching to come back into herself. In her email to me, she wrote:

> I'm a survivor of the Boston Marathon bombing. I never had an issue with anxiety or panic prior to that event. But man, when it hits you—it hits hard.
>
> I crossed the finish line at exactly the time of the first bombing. I was thirty feet from the explosion. The second

> bomb exploded right near two of my friends who were cheering me on.
>
> Disoriented, on the ground, and oddly calm—I knew the girls were in the smoke or beyond the smoke. I knew something bad happened. I thought we were all going to die and that maybe they already had.
>
> The scene looked like a war zone. My friends were alive but terribly injured. You can imagine the sequence of events. From the hospital through the court trial—it was all a horror show.
>
> I had always been a runner. I ran and ran and ran. But now, the disconnect between my mind and body is enormous. I am exhausted, despite trying so hard to relax. I struggle to sleep. I struggle to breathe. The experience and guilt have become a haunting ghost.

This first contact led to a series of emails between us. When we met in person and began to work together, one thing was immediately clear: Meghan was locked in a state of high alert. Her nervous system was armoring against a perpetual experience of *not feeling safe*. She wanted to relax, but she *couldn't*.

Meghan needed to begin with her nervous system and re-learn how to sense support underneath her body.

A New Relationship

The blog post that Meghan read was about one of the most pivotal moments in my life, losing my sister-in-law to cancer. This event, and facing my own fundamental vulnerability in the world, rattled me to my core. It also exposed me to buried fears, which I had harbored in my body all my life. In addition to the panic attacks, it altered my self-view as a person in total control of her life. I was a mind-over-matter achiever. I was the person who thought anxiety or depression was a choice. And then I came to personally know anxiety and how it can make you believe that you are genuinely falling apart.

After my year of total breakdown, I began building a new relationship with my anxiety by teaching myself to remember my relationship with support (in this case, the literal ground).

Through my yoga and meditation practice, I already had a tangible understanding of *grounding.* I had learned how to sense my body on the earth and have a bodily experience of being held up by the physical, tactile support underneath me. And through my own healing, I developed a practice that begins with building a foundation we can return to—one that allows us to feel supported and held. This foundation is essential for cultivating a sense of safety, both within our nervous system and in our lives.

As I thought about Meghan's experience, it got me thinking more deeply about how we can sense support when the very ground we are walking on is not safe. Where do we start when we just can't feel our connection to support, when we don't feel safe enough to rest on what is underneath us? What do we do when our nervous system is *stuck* in "fight, flight, or freeze"?

Meghan longed to come back into her body and let herself land on the ground—to remember the support that was there, holding her up. But how? For her, the ground was inherently unsafe.

The main entry point for this work begins with establishing *physical* safety. But this can be complicated when we consider the variety of stories we each have about our relationship to our environment. Many of us have not—whether currently or in the past—truly felt safe in our physical spaces for various reasons. These may include domestic or community violence, laws that threaten our humanity, natural disasters, war, or even a bomb exploding at the finish line of a race.

This practice, while honoring our relationship with both past and present conditions of the surrounding environment, also invites us to connect with the physical ground beneath us.

Even if only for one breath.

While we often can't control the conditions of our environment, we can learn to relate to whatever tactile support is physically under our body in a given moment. This is the first line of communication with our nervous system.

We establish communication with our nervous system by sending the message that, in this moment—right here, right now—we are supported. Allowing the brain to register this is how we begin to foster a sense of safety. The big takeaway here is that we begin our practice of sensing safety—in and through the body—with whatever our conditions are.

Carry On

Creating a sense of safety and learning to receive support are interconnected practices. As we build trust in one, the other naturally grows alongside it, making both safety and support essential elements to cultivate together.

When we talk about how to communicate safety to the brain, it's helpful to look at the behavior of babies, and the primal and primary ways they receive the message that they are safe.

Imagine the way a baby is soothed. A main way to calm an agitated or crying infant, a caretaker picks them up and carries them. Babies are neurobiologically wired to stop crying when carried. The calming response to being held is an evolutionary design, helping our species survive.

Research confirms this to be a universal phenomenon. As the mother of an uber-colicky infant, I, too, can confirm this. In fact, for three consecutive (very long) years, the only way Willow would calm was by being carried. I remember reading about how swaddling (firmly wrapping a cloth around the baby, creating a womb-like encompassment) can support the nervous system's regulation, offering some relief to parents like me whose infants needed continual carrying. The snug pressure of the cloth communicates to the infant's brain that they are being held, which creates a somatic sense of safety, triggering a relaxation response that helps break the cycle of dysregulation.

Feeling Held, or Not

While swaddling mimics the sensation of being held, researchers found that the calming response relies specifically on tactile input and proprioception.

Proprioception is the ability to sense, feel, experience, and track our body's position in space. For example, it enables a person to close their eyes and touch their nose with their index finger. It allows us to feel whether our feet are on soft grass or hard cement without looking, even while wearing shoes. Proprioception is how we begin to trust that we can *sense* the ground underneath us *and* feel that it is *holding us up*.

Proprioception is impaired when we are stressed. During states of anxiety, it's common to feel "out of our body" or disoriented. We might also experience sensations like spaciness or the feeling of falling or flying, along with physical symptoms such as vertigo. When we are stressed, we simply cannot *feel* grounded.

Our proprioception may be inhibited for many reasons, from continual low-lying stress to exposure to trauma. In addition, injuries and a wide variety of medical and neurological conditions can all lessen our ability to feel our body's connection to support, thereby diminishing our ability to *feel held.*

The feeling of being unsupported and unsafe makes us continually react to the present moment—as well as all our interactions within those moments—from a stance in which we feel the need to protect ourselves. We react from a place where we are still fighting or fleeing.

And, even if we were born feeling held, swaddled, and safe, many of us, as we grow and move through the stressors of life, can lose connection with this sense of support, both around us and underneath us.

Learning to Land

There are two aspects of learning to Land. The first is learning to remember or recognize that there is support (in fact, a whole planet) under our body. But then, we must also learn to allow ourselves to physically rest on that support, to give our weight to it. Allowing ourselves to be supported *is how we shift* into a state where we can Pause.

I began this process with Meghan by exploring restorative yoga—a slow, mindful practice focused on reducing effort and tension by allowing the ground and props to support you. Meghan eventually came to love Surfboard Pose, where you lie belly-down, the front of your body on props like blankets and bolsters. This complete contact with the ground mimics the sensation of being swaddled to our nervous system. While we can't wrap ourselves up like babies whenever we feel anxious, this pose comes pretty close.

When you can sense that your whole front body is in contact with the ground, it's easier to relax and eventually release into the earth's support. Over time, Meghan allowed the props to hold her up. She no longer felt like she was "floating" in her body. These feelings of safety did not happen overnight, but she gradually began to let herself be supported. For Meghan, this was where the process of truly Landing began.

Don't worry. I'm not suggesting we lie face-down every time we face a challenging conversation with our teen or partner—there is no need to face-plant to feel supported! But it's important to understand these concepts to see why the Pause must start in the body. Calming ourselves begins with the body. Feeling grounded has to come from the body first.

While a physical practice like yoga can be a great way to connect with and sense our *relationship* with the ground, we don't need yoga or props to experience the tactile support beneath our body right now. A chair, couch, bed, the ground, the earth—learning to land is something we can practice anytime, anywhere. It's available to us all the time, wherever we are. I often practice while in the middle of a conversation (especially a difficult one), while in line at the grocery store, when I'm driving or stuck in traffic, at the airport, and even while watching the news.

Whether you're sitting, lying down, driving, or walking, take a moment to notice the support beneath you. Can you feel where your seat, feet, or back meets the surface holding you? Pause and allow yourself to settle into that support, feeling your body gently held in this moment.

As we build a new relationship with the ground beneath us, we become more aware of what it feels like to be ungrounded. This awareness is one of the most valuable skills we can develop, as staying grounded isn't a constant state. The goal isn't to remain grounded forever, but to recognize when we've lost our footing and gently guide ourselves back to a sense of support—if only for a single breath.

Landing is a practice we can rely on for life. Even if it's the only practice we commit to, it will profoundly support our nervous system and guide us toward inner calm.

Landing is the foundation we need to feel safe enough to Pause.

If we want to feel safe, we begin with learning to sense support.

We return to remember the ground underneath our bodies.

We remember there is a whole Earth underneath us.

We welcome ourselves back home, into our body, on the Earth; on our life partner the Earth.

Again and again.

Sensing Support: A Pre-Practice Inquiry

Take a moment to notice what's under your body. Maybe it is a chair, a couch, the floor, the earth. Sense where your seat or feet meet support. *Feel* the support underneath you. You might even touch it with your hand if it is helpful.

Can you allow the support that is under your body to hold you up more?

For just one breath, can you allow your full body weight to be held up by the support underneath your body?

What does it feel like to be held up?

What does it feel like, in your body, when you can fully rely on support?

PAUSE TO PRACTICE LANDING

This short practice is always where we begin, as it forms the very foundation of the Pause. You can also use it on its own anytime you need to feel more grounded. Since it is only six breaths long, feel free to repeat it as many times as you like.

- To begin, bring to mind the image of an hourglass that was just turned upside down, sand emptying from top to bottom. Imagine your body as an hourglass. On your next three exhales, let all the weighty "sand" drain from your upper body down into your lower body:
- As you exhale, let all the heaviness drain down from your head, neck, and shoulders. Allow your inhale to flow into you on its own.
- As you exhale, feel the "sand" draining from your shoulders and chest down into your belly. Allow your inhale to expand your whole chest.
- As you exhale, allow all the sandiness to flow down from your belly into your pelvis, legs, and feet. Feel your feet (or seat, or back), heavy, spreading on the earth. Welcome your inhale as it comes back to fill you again.
- Let your body rest entirely, completely, on the support under you. Let your shoulders rest on your body. Let the earth hold you up.

Again.

- Exhaling, feel the weight drain down from your head, neck, and shoulders.

- Exhaling, all the heaviness releases from your shoulders and chest down into your belly.
- Exhaling, release the weight of your belly, pelvis, and legs, down into the ground.
- Enjoy a full complete breath as you let yourself Land, completely, in the spot where you are. Here. Now.

To close, set an intention to stay aware of the ground supporting you, as you expand your awareness back into the space around you and move into your next moment.

Please note that most of the practices in this book can be done sitting, standing, or even lying down—whichever position feels most supportive for you. For some of us, settling into stillness—even for a few breaths—can be especially challenging when anxiety is present. In those moments, if you need additional care for your nervous system, you'll find a range of helpful practices in Chapter 15. Alternatively, you may wish to explore Landing while moving by trying the Mindful Walking practice on pages 231–33, which can be a healing option when grounding and centering are needed but stillness feels out of reach.

May you allow yourself to Land
in the spot where you are,
just as you are.
Here, now.

CHAPTER 4

Arrive

KRISTEN WAS FORTY-EIGHT years old when she first came to my class. A few sessions into our work together, she shared that she lived most of her life with low-lying anxiety. She grew up with a sick mother who was most often bedridden. Kristen constantly worried that things could fall apart at any moment. She worked hard in all areas of her life to feel in control. But that quest escalated after one tragic evening during her junior year in college.

It was a warm fall night and Kristen and a couple of friends were getting a late-night snack at a fast-food restaurant. Just as they sat on a bench to eat, they were approached by three men who held them up at gunpoint. It all happened so quickly; her friend was shot point-blank and died. In the years following this tragedy, Kristen had to testify at three murder trials. And in the decades since, she has struggled with chronic anxiety and panic attacks.

After years of therapy, Kristen wanted to incorporate more somatic healing modalities to help find relief in her body and mind. Her self-healing quest brought her to me.

Kristen shared that on any day at any time, she could be overcome by high anxiety in a millisecond. "I jump out of my skin when my doorbell rings, feel panicky from loud unexpected sounds, and terrified when I'm walking outside in the dark."

There were days when she even confused her stress symptoms with a severe health emergency. "Sometimes I felt like I was having a heart attack; I would get a stabbing pain in my chest and struggle breathing."

Hypervigilance was exhausting her. And she told me that after a period of high stress, her energy would get extremely low. "I would actually feel physically ill, like I was coming down with the flu," she said.

Kristen was oscillating between the instinct to fight, the urge to flee, and the impulse to freeze. As we worked together, she became aware of how her anxiety was making her feel. "My mind is always racing. My scary thoughts make me so tense. I hold my breath, my hands are in fists, my glutes are gripped. My throat constricts as if I am being strangled. I want to scream and run away as fast as possible. And sometimes I want to curl up in a ball and hide under a blanket."

Even though Kristen had loving intentions, she confessed that her anxiety took a toll on her relationships, explicitly affecting those she loved most: "I often find myself arguing easily with family members—trying to control them to keep them safe. I want to be more at ease and present. I just don't know how to get there. And, maybe, I'm also scared of the present."

I share Kristen's story because it captures the struggle of her nervous system being unable to rest in the present moment and the feeling of being imprisoned by relentless rumination. While most of us won't experience trauma of this magnitude, all of us will encounter anxiety or stress, which may become chronic at some point in our lives.

Our fight-or-flight response is continually triggered by a wide range of real and imagined threats, leaving most of us with a persistent sense of vulnerability. We get stuck in this stress loop—and the more the mind races away, fast-forwarding into the future or rewinding into the past, getting activated and triggered, the more the body follows. The more the body follows, the less we can be present in the moment as it is. This state can arise from a number of different circumstances, all equally valid, and the strategies to work with it are universal.

Arrive on the Breath

We often find ourselves caught up in worries of the day—about relationships, finances, work, or even the weather. Hardships like illness, loss, and grief are unavoidable, but what makes them even more challenging is the constant barrage of thoughts and emotions we layer *on top* of them.

Our primal need to protect ourselves, fueled by stress hormones, keeps us locked in cycles of worry. We run from task to task, distracting ourselves with technology or to-do lists, or anything else that will keep us from experiencing what is presently happening in our bodies or lives.

How, then, do we break free and return to the moment that we are in right now?

Like Landing, the first step is through the body. We begin by sensing the support beneath us, then shift our attention to the breath. Through this, we create more calm and the conditions for safety and presence.

When Kristen got caught in her intrusive thoughts, her body followed. Her breaths grew short, shallow, and quick, which, when in a threatening situation, is essential to instantly energize the body. This helps us get the oxygen and energy needed to power our ability to fight or flee. But it is not helpful when we want or need to be calm and grounded. In fact, it is quite the opposite.

The tighter and more shallow our breath cycle, the more it perpetuates messages to the brain that we need to actively protect ourselves, keeping us in a state of low-level, or even high-level, anxiety. This, too, is what happened with Kristen. And this is the state that many of us live in all the time.

There are so many reasons why our breath becomes restricted. Our stressful thoughts minimize our breath. Emotions affect our breathing: We hold our breath when we're sad, angry, or scared. Also, tension in our bodies and muscles (like the psoas) affects our breathing. Our posture affects our breath, too; air cannot come and go easily when our chest slumps, collapses, or even puffs up. Our breathing becomes physiologically obstructed, which physically and neurologically inhibits our ability to feel grounded and calm. And this makes the present feel like an uncertain, scary place.

When we are in "fight, flight, or freeze," our reactions to *whatever* comes our way are limited to three behavior categories: aggression, avoidance, or withdrawal. And most of this occurs without our conscious awareness.

So, how do we Arrive in the present when we constantly feel unsafe?

Our Breathing Switch

Arriving is the act of interrupting our stress response with a deep, full, slow breath. We are training in Landing and Arriving so that when we find ourselves hijacked by fear and stress, we can regulate ourselves.

Deep, full, slow breathing is tied to our relaxation response. The relaxation response is governed by the parasympathetic nervous system, which, in addition to helping calm our mind, brings our body back to a regulated state and returns all the essential systems—like heart rate, blood pressure, digestion, immunity, and respiration—to a state where they are running more optimally for health and healing. These systems get their "instructions" *from* the state of the nervous system.

Unfortunately, we cannot influence these systems just by saying to ourselves, "Heart rate, slow down" or "Digestion, calm down and get more efficient." We can talk to most of our bodily systems until we are blue in the face, and not much will happen.

However, there is one system that we *can manually* override—the breath. And when we override that system, it, in turn, affects *all* our other essential systems.

Paying attention to the breath is the fastest way to shift out of a cycle of fear and into a state where we feel more centered.

When we breathe more deeply and fully, we grow calmer. While a state of calm doesn't make all our problems go away, it does give us more control over our ability to think more clearly and to be more discerning. When we take deep, full breaths, we can calm the stress response, move toward a more flexible nervous system, and be more mindful about how we respond.

As we take a deep conscious breath, on purpose, we prime the nervous system to shift into the relaxation response and Arrive in the present.

A Bear Story

A few summers ago, I led a retreat at Kripalu in the Berkshire Mountains of Massachusetts. It was just before sunset, and I was on my way to the lake for a twilight dip, accompanied by five dear friends who were assisting me with the retreat. As we strolled down the sprawling front lawn, a long slope of tall summer grasses adorned with wildflowers, butterflies, and fireflies, it felt like the perfect summer evening.

At the bottom of the hill, we came upon the lake path, which was too narrow to fit all six of us across, so we slowed to shift our configuration. Walking in pairs, surrounded by the dense cool woods, our chatting blended into the symphony of the deeper forest soundscape—buzzing, crackling, and birdsong.

Amber suddenly tilted her head, asking, "Did you hear that?"

"I heard it," Nicole said, her voice edged with concern.

"What? What was it?" I asked, my words tumbling out, barely masking my nerves.

"That!" Amber exclaimed, pointing in the direction of the sound.

I caught the sharp sound of bushes crashing just as a bear burst through, seemingly out of nowhere. I saw it lunge toward us, but I was already running before its feet hit the ground. And I'm not even sure I saw it land on the path. I doubt any of us did.

That is, except for Amber.

I was running like . . . well, like I had just seen a huge scary bear.

Amber stood her ground.

Heart pounding, audibly panting, I could barely hear Amber's voice calling out firmly, "Stop running. Turn around. Arms up. Stop running. Turn around. Arms up."

I'm not sure how many times she repeated this or exactly how long it was before I turned around, but it must not have been too long because as I stopped running and turned around, I could see the bear running down the path. *Away from us.*

At this point, we runners were standing tall, arms up and grounded, but definitely still freaked out.

Authoritatively, Amber said, "We need to get out of here; the mother must be nearby—she'll be looking for her cub."

"Cub?! That bear was *huge*!" Nicole exclaimed.

"That *was* Mama!" Patrizia insisted.

"*Definitely*, Mama!" I confirmed.

Amber remained steady. "That was a cub. Which means Mama must be near. We don't want to run into her. She'll be aggressive if she's looking for her cub."

While we couldn't agree on whether it was a cub, we all knew one thing for sure—we needed to get out of there. We walked the rest of the way to the lake with our arms up, acting big and talking loudly to let any bears that might be listening know we were coming through.

With more mindful steps, our breathing began to steady.

When we got to the lake, Amber called the Front Desk, who told us to stay where we were and sent a Security Guard to pick us up.

On the ride back, the relaxed guard—humored by our "city style"—said, "You never can be sure exactly what you'll need to do when you see a bear. But you'll always have to be able to stay calm."

Being six yoga teachers, we had a great laugh about that.

Out of the Woods

When Amber was grounded, she could breathe deeply and stay calm. She could see the bear running *away* from us and also could see, from her perspective, that we were not in any danger from *that* bear.

Being grounded, Landing, calming herself, breathing, and Arriving in the present moment enabled Amber to keep her wits about herself and choose her next move. A perfect example of Pausing.

With her prefrontal cortex switched ON, she could use her thinking mind to predict that danger could still be lurking—a Mama looking for her cub. She could also steadily guide us out of danger while remaining "bear-aware."

Amber had the extra benefit of being *trained* to respond to a bear, which helped her remember exactly what to do. Amber's ability to Pause in this situation was like muscle memory.

All of this is important to know—that being able to Land, to stop for a moment and feel the ground, that having the muscle memory of knowing to take a breath in the face of something that *seems* threatening (maybe it is, maybe it isn't, we can't stop to think about it!)—is the foundation for being able to meet a situation from a place of wisdom and clarity.

While the rest of us initially ran, we also were able to stop ourselves. To Land. To breathe and Arrive. This is pausing, too. It didn't happen as fast as it happened for Amber. But it was available to us very quickly. We could self-regulate in seconds and return to a state where we could make a better choice, a new response.

We encounter circumstances daily that can *seem* threatening (at least I do), and developing this muscle memory is critical in our ability to assess a situation accurately. Or generously. Or with compassion.

How Do We Develop Muscle Memory?

We begin with Landing. The more we're able to feel our relationship to our support, the more grounded we feel. The more grounded we feel, the more we are able to take a conscious deep breath. Think of it like building any muscle—it takes practice and repetition. We do this even when we're not in a stressful situation, so that the nervous system has it as an option when we are threatened. The practice is reminding ourselves to Land and Arrive. Again and again.

When I want to create a new habit, I remind myself by setting an alarm every two hours and taking a small break to practice. I also Pause before each meal and when I brush my teeth in the morning—coupling a new practice with an old routine. Setting times during the day to repeat the steps has helped make it a natural habit.

Each time we Land and connect with the ground, we shift toward calm. This sets the foundation for Pausing and deeper breaths, helping us regulate the nervous system, and making it easier to access when needed.

To Land: Feel your feet on the ground.

To Arrive: Consciously allow a deeper breath.

Repeating these steps again and again is how we build our muscle memory.

Repeating these steps again and again changes everything.

The Muscle—and the Nerve—to Pause

Let's take a closer look at how our body and brain communicate through the breath. At the core of this connection lies one essential muscle: the diaphragm. Many of us know it as the muscle of breathing—a thin, dome-shaped muscle that sits below the lungs and heart, attaches to the sternum and all along the bottom of the rib cage and spine. By contracting and relaxing, it draws our breath into the lungs and moves it out. Below it sits all our abdominal organs, which facilitate digestion and elimination.

But the diaphragm's function isn't just physiological; it plays a crucial role in calming the nervous system and anchoring us in the present moment. This muscle in our body has *everything* to do with our mental state. It is directly related to our thoughts and feelings.

Remember how the psoas runs from the inner thigh, behind the organs in the gut, and merges with the spine at the diaphragm? Well, when the diaphragm is constricted, it can chronically restrict breathing. Many things cause such constriction, including being in an acute or chronic state of fear or stress—running around as if our life depended on it. The whole body grows rigid in the stress response, including the spine, the belly, the psoas, and the diaphragm, which connects to it all. In short, when our body is tense, our diaphragm has less range of motion.

When we are not in the stress response, the diaphragm should move rhythmically and continually, and most of the time, involuntarily. Breathing is designed to happen on its own; we don't *need* to consciously suck air in or push air out (thank goodness!). That's part of the reptilian brain's job. Breathing keeps going no matter what state we are in—asleep, awake, happy, or sad. This is very helpful to remember. While we can manually override the quality of the breath, we don't *do* the actual breathing. Yes, we are always breathing, but I like to think of it as: *we are always being breathed*.

However, when we learn to take deep, intentional breaths on purpose, it helps us shift from a restricted shallow breathing pattern to one that encourages more complete breaths. This, in turn, facilitates the relaxation response.

The diaphragm has another partner in this job, in addition to the psoas. When it moves slowly and rhythmically, allowing for complete inhalations and exhalations, it also stimulates the vagus nerve and massages the abdominal organs.

The vagus nerve is the single most important nerve for calming ourselves. It runs between the gut and the brain, passing through the diaphragm on the way. This nerve is the actual "switch" that initiates the relaxation response via the nervous system.

In short, the less freely the diaphragm moves, the less easily we breathe, the less the vagus nerve gets stimulated, and the more anxious we feel. In contrast, the more we ground and center ourselves, the deeper we can breathe, stimulating the vagus nerve and signaling the brain to down-regulate (calm) our overstimulated systems. Full, deep, natural breathing sends messages to the brain that we are safe—which deepens the relaxation response, helping us Arrive here, now.

The Ever-Changing Now

We often overlook the fact that the present moment—"the now"—is inherently fluid and ever-changing, with one moment seamlessly flowing into the next. So, if every moment is fresh and new, how do we create a feeling of being grounded when things are always changing?

We tend to think of "grounding" as the act of creating stable conditions. And we tend to think that the opposite of being grounded is being out of control. So, if we can just get "grounded"—get things stable—we will be okay. We will have control.

But the truth is, nothing stays stable. Nothing stays the same. Everything is constantly changing. The nature of all things *is* change.

We know there will always be things we can't control. We cannot control the weather. We cannot control when a bear jumps—seemingly out of nowhere—onto our path. We're wired to want control and safety in our lives. But even if we do manage to achieve stability for periods of time, we know that everything can be pulled out from underneath us at any moment. Yet, no matter how much we know this all to be true, our nervous system is still always trying to keep things *the same.*

To truly Pause, we need to *feel* grounded, regardless of whether things are actually steady, stable, or solid. Rather than trying to avoid the groundless *feeling* of uncertainty, we learn to return our awareness to feeling the support under our body. To grow conscious of our breathing. To Arrive *here*, even *with* our shaky feelings.

When Amber saw the bear, she didn't try to make the outside world stable; she made her inside world steady so that she could meet the unpredictable conditions of the outer world and, in this case, respond to the potential threat. Amber grounded *herself* so she could respond to what was actually happening in the present moment. The present is the *only* place we can respond to what is actually happening.

Arriving on the breath helps us gather our attention and feel more centered. It helps us feel more integrated and present. More calm and open.

Shepherding Ourselves Back

There is no magical day when we will always be grounded and present.

While consciously tuning into your breath helps you stay calm and present, the reality is, we can't maintain that awareness every moment. Our minds aren't wired to stay with the breath continuously.

We each have our own personal histories of feeling safe or holding trauma. And due to our particular stress and tension, we don't stay aware of our breath all the time, nor do we stay present all the time. Rather, we are designed to look for what we should "worry" about that may be coming in the future—or think about how we should have done something different in the past. Most of us will rarely remain present for even a single breath before the mind runs away, rewinding into the past or fast-forwarding into the future. Our mind will continually be pulled away. And as our mind is pulled away, our body instinctively tenses in response.

The solution is to become aware when we're no longer present. Notice when your breath becomes short and shallow. Recognize when you're holding your breath. Tune in when you realize you're not grounded in the moment.

(Please consider that when working with trauma, PTSD, or long-standing nervous system conditions, it can be beneficial to work with a trained therapist.)

Arriving means noticing when we're resisting our breath and gently guiding ourselves back to Land, breathing more deeply each time. It's about building the habit of remembering—again and again—to *return to the breath.* One breath at a time. And if we have to do it a hundred times a day, or a hundred times an hour, that is the practice. That is totally okay. And normal!

I've been training in noticing my breath for over thirty years. And I've learned that we are training in *returning* to the breath, *not* staying with the breath.

Each time we gently guide ourselves back to the breath—without judging, or blaming, or berating ourselves—we strengthen our ability to return more easily the next time. And as we expand our capacity to Land and Arrive, we also expand our capacity to Pause.

Back to Kristen

After our first encounter, Kristen studied with me for a long time and eventually became one of my community's assistant teachers and mentors. Over the years, she taught LAR-LAR in my classes, but more importantly, she shared how LAR-LAR has changed her life.

Kristen explains that by practicing several times a day during calm moments, she strengthens her ability to remember these techniques when faced with challenges or triggers.

She says, "Because I practice Pausing regularly, I don't escalate as easily. Or when I do escalate, I'm able to return more quickly to the ground below me, and to my breathing. I am definitely more aware of how I feel. Which also helps me be more aware of how I'm interacting with myself and others. It's changed me, and all my relationships."

Like Kristen, we begin to change our mindless habitual reactions by developing muscle memory. Each time we calm ourselves—Land and then Arrive—we set conditions to calm ourselves again, more quickly and more easily.

The Free-Flowing Breath

We Arrive here, now, on the actual flow of the breath. We tune into our breath throughout the day because it's a powerful tool that calms us and anchors our attention in the present moment. After all, the breath only exists in the now.

Notice your next in-breath. The inhale is happening now. Right now. As you follow it, you can stay with this moment as it is happening.

Notice your next out-breath. The exhale is only happening now. As you follow it with your awareness, you flow along with the ever-new, now moment.

The breath is always here, guiding you to the now. *The breath is the metronome of now.*

Being here, now, is where we can respond to whatever is happening. It is the *only* place we can respond to what is *actually* happening.

The breath only exists in the now.

The breath is the metronome of now.

Just Noticing: A Pre-Practice Inquiry

Take a moment to turn your attention to your breathing. What do you notice? Maybe you notice that you hadn't been aware of your breath until I asked you to check in. What is the quality of your breath? Don't try to change it. Is it short and shallow? Deep and slow? Somewhere in between these two? No judgment. Just notice. We are simply noticing how things are.

PAUSE TO PRACTICE ARRIVING

This short practice helps us to ground and then shift further into calm and presence. It has a powerful impact in just a few breaths, however, feel free to repeat it as many times as you like.

- To begin, bring your attention to what is underneath your body. Notice where your body meets support. Let your body rest on that support. Let yourself Land here, in the spot, right where you are. Stay grounded as you turn your attention to your breath. Expand your awareness of the air around you.
- On your next inhale, mentally trace the path of the air, the breath, as it moves from outside your body, in through your nostrils, down into your lungs. Allow the breath to fill—to Arrive in you. Continue to stay present with the breath, mentally tracing the flow of your breath as it moves from inside your body, back out into the space around you.
- On your next inhalation, allow your mind to rest on the flow of your breath as you follow it into your body. On your exhalation, simply rest your attention on the wave of the breath flowing out, returning to join the ocean of air around you. Let your mind Arrive on your breath.
- Noticing how it flows in and out on its own. *Feel* your next breath Arriving in your body. Stay present *with* the breath as it flows back out.

Again.

- Inhaling, trace your breath as it flows in. Follow your breath as it flows out.

- Inhaling, feel your breath Arriving in your body. Exhaling, feel your whole body softening.
- Inhaling, let your mind flow along with your breath. Exhaling, rest your mind on your breath.

Stay with the breath as you expand your awareness to simultaneously notice the support under your body. Let your body rest on the support.

Half of your awareness is on the ground. Half of your awareness is on the breath.

Imagine an hourglass, the bottom half filled with sand—grounded—the top half clear and open.

Imagine your body like an hourglass. Let your bottom half rest on the earth. Land. Let the breath flow through the clear upper hourglass of you.

Allow your mind to Arrive on your breath. Here. Now. Just as you are.

To close, set an intention to stay aware of the ground supporting you and your breath flowing through you, as you expand your awareness back into the space around you and move into your next moment.

We are always being supported by our life partners, the earth and the breath.

May you Arrive home,
on your breath,
into the present moment.
Here, now.

CHAPTER 5

Relax

So, WHAT DOES relaxation really mean?

Relaxation is often viewed as the opposite of work—just taking a break, lying on the couch, or watching TV. It's frequently seen as wasting time or even as a synonym for laziness.

It's true that getting a massage or lying on a beach can be relaxing. But to understand Relaxation, we first need to understand how we are not Relaxed; the truth is, this has to do with our body *and* our mind.

The neurological state of relaxation is defined as "the state of being free from tension and anxiety." This explanation points us back to discussing how to move from the state of the stress response to the relaxation response.

So, we will reflect on what happens in our bodies when we are stressed.

Our First Responder

As you'll recall from Chapter 3, the brain developed in three basic stages: reptilian (brain stem), mammalian (limbic system), and primate (cortex). The older area of the brain, specifically the reptilian brain, is the fastest responder to threats. It's our First Responder.

Let me back up a moment to revisit the fact that looking for danger, that go-to, habitual instinct we have, is not a character flaw. It is the nature of the nervous system, the mind, and our conditioning. It is our evolutionary design. The earliest threat our First Responder instinctively protected us from was pain, which, in ancient times, often meant the danger of being eaten, maimed, or starved.

As humans, we face our first threats when we are infants and cannot survive independently. These threats include not being fed when hungry or being ignored when needing comfort and connection. To a baby, everything is a matter of survival.

So, as creatures programmed to avoid pain, our First Responder sounds an alarm in the face of anything that could cause us *any* kind of pain. In fact, the part of our brain that perceives physical pain is the same part of our brain that perceives emotional pain. The First Responder does not differentiate between the two. It protects us in the exact same way from either. Whether it's the threat of a bear or the discomfort of entering a room full of strangers, our First Responder triggers the same alarm.

As you can imagine, we fire a lot of alarms as we experience many different kinds of pain in our lives, from physical to emotional. I love how Buddhist meditation teacher Ethan Nichtern puts it: "Inhabiting a human nervous system is kind of like living in a house where the doorbell and the burglar alarm make exactly the same sound."

Of course, some of our alarms are essential for us to protect ourselves in the world. But this system often misfires. And when alarms are going off in our midst, all day, every day—or even just once in a while—we behave in a very predictable way: We instantly get tense.

Our old friend, the stress response, activates to support our survival, giving us all the resources we need to fight, flee, or freeze. Our muscles tense to help us run, punch, kick, or curl up in a ball to play dead. Tensing happens instantaneously—not only for power, but also to serve as armor to protect our organs from blows of pain and loss of blood. This protective stance becomes our tension.

Tension—Our First Line of Defense

Many of us describe our contracted muscles, the feeling of being bound up in our body, as "tightness." Often, the words "tension" and "tightness" are used interchangeably. However, they are worth differentiating.

Tightness describes muscular contractions from activities like lifting weights, running, carrying groceries, gardening, or even prolonged postures like sitting or typing. After our muscles have exerted effort for these activities, they may shorten in length and cause us to feel sore or uncomfortable. We may find relief once we stretch these muscles back to their resting length.

Tension is the body's way of protecting itself by contracting muscles in response to perceived vulnerability. Whether the threat is physical or emotional, real or imagined, our muscles tense up to form a protective shield. Instantly, when our fear circuitry is triggered, our muscles tense to help us survive an acute threat. This response is what happens when we need to run from a python. But our muscles also tense simply from *imagining* an acute threat, like a python that is not *actually* there. Tension also builds from hearing the latest *news*, ruminating about the *news of the past*, or imagining future news.

Tension is the way our body responds to feeling unsafe or provoked. Again, tension arises from *anything* threatening us; meaning, if we feel excluded, left out, separated, or unloved, our body responds with protective mechanisms.

Every time we get messages (from others or ourselves) that things are uncertain, unsafe, or somehow not right, we tense.

This response—the clenching of our jaw, hiking up our shoulders, gripping our bellies, holding our breath—that initially developed for our safety can become a pattern—a habit in our bodies and our lives. And often, we don't even know we feel this way until we discover it. This habitual tension we live with keeps the stress response firing, and keeps us armoring ourselves up.

Like our feeling ungrounded, like our short, shallow breath, a tense body continually sends messages to the brain to "tense more"—and this tension stands between us and our ability to Relax, often inhibiting our ability to Pause.

Remember: The relaxation response is the opposite of our stress response. It is how our body calms down and returns to homeostasis after stress. When we are more grounded, breathing deeply, and able to ease our tension, the relaxation response initiates, and hormones are released to bring our body and mind back to a state of equilibrium, allowing us to be physically relaxed and mentally alert simultaneously.

This cocktail of chemical messengers—serotonin, oxytocin, dopamine, and endorphins—acts on our organs and tissue to control everything from how our body functions to how we feel.

These chemicals promote clarity, connection, creativity, and even compassion. Commonly nicknamed the "feel-good hormones" because they act on our brain to generate uplifting emotions—such as euphoria, contentment, or joy—they also relate to our feelings of safety and trust.

We are simply not wired to Relax if we don't feel supported. When we feel supported, we feel more safe. When we allow our bodies to be held up, we don't have to do so much work to hold ourselves up.

Willow and Barbie

When Willow was five, she couldn't stand being apart from me. She often asked me to go with her to the next room to get something she needed. And she always needed something.

At first, I would just make accommodations and do my work in her room. I tried to pad each room with extra toys and things to keep Willow busy. But still, what she really wanted and *needed* always seemed to be in a different room. What *Barbie needed* was a different dress, different shoes, a different bag, a different Barbie friend. These things were *always* in a different room.

On some days, I'd be impatient: "You have so many outfits for Barbie *here*. Find something for her *here*."

And there were other days when I would engage Willow in conversation, trying to get to the root of her fear. But honestly, I think I was more motivated by getting her "over" this thing, and I'd try to convince her that there was *nothing* to be afraid of.

Exasperated, I'd try to urge her to go on her own—or, more accurately, push her. "There is nothing to be scared of. Just relax and go get what you need," I'd say.

As you might expect, this approach did not work. Willow would invariably tense up more, responding to some alarm inside her—one that neither she nor I could explain.

She stood, clutching her Barbie, knuckles white with her petrified grip. She was in a frozen state. This is one of the many manifestations of our alarm. It is in our body. No amount of convincing could move Willow. Because, for whatever reason, she did not feel safe. She *wanted* to get her stuff, but she *couldn't.*

Again, we tense in the face of something that feels threatening—real or imagined. We may not even know exactly what is making us tense, but we become contracted, unable to move freely and flexibly. However, once we know that we are carrying tension, we can start working with our nervous system in a whole new way.

How We Meet Tension

Whenever I told Willow to "relax," my life got decidedly worse. In addition to her insistent and unrelenting questions about when I would be done, she would invariably start a little drama, with her Barbies talking to each other two feet away, leaving me to listen to a furious Barbie acting out how awful I was. Needless to say, we were both tense.

Tension is how our body responds to feeling stressed, unsafe, and provoked. Tension acts as our personal bodyguard, a form of defensive protection. It's the stress response taking root in our body. But tension can only soften and release in a safe, supportive environment.

For this reason, the way we meet our tension matters.

One day, when I felt especially relaxed, Willow asked me to go get Barbie's dress from upstairs.

I Paused and remembered what it felt like to be anxious. Scared. Terrified, actually.

It was during my year of panic attacks. I was invited to Australia for a work event. But my anxiety left me with a staunch fear of flying. In fact, during that time, it wasn't only flying—I could not get in a subway, found it hard to drive a car on the highway, and on some days, I could barely even leave my apartment.

But going to Australia was a bucket-list trip for me. I didn't know how I could do it, but I also couldn't imagine passing it up.

So, I worked with my therapist, who helped me develop a new "relationship" with my fear by paying attention to what fear felt like in my body.

Fear felt like clenching my jaw, hiking up my shoulders, holding my breath, and feeling absolute resistance to the moment. So, each time I noticed I was doing those things, I reminded myself that I was just experiencing a *feeling of fear.*

I created the mantra "Fear is here" to help me acknowledge my body's reaction without falling into my typical anxiety loop. This simple phrase reminded me to observe the presence of my fear, rather than add more fear to the moment.

As I repeated the mantra, I consciously felt my feet on the ground. I expanded my awareness to my breath. Breathing deeply, I began systematically going to my chronic areas of tension and softening them. Three breaths—each exhale dropping my shoulders, unclenching my jaw, unfurling my fists. This practice is what helped me get on the plane to Australia.

This is where the first LAR in LAR-LAR was truly put to the test—the ritual of grounding myself by feeling my feet, breathing deeply, and intentionally relaxing.

To my good fortune, once on the plane, an open seat was next to me. And, as I clicked my seatbelt in, quietly repeating my mantra, "Fear is here," I considered giving both my fear and myself a little more space.

I said, "Hello, Fear. I know you are here. You can not only come with me; you can have your own seat. You can fly here next to me."

I imagined Fear settling into 22B and putting on its own little seatbelt. I know this may sound silly, but my fear, which was an integral part of me moments ago, was now just another passenger on this long flight across the world. Fear and I flew side by side to Australia. And both of us had a lot more space.

Since then, I've used this tool countless times—likely every day.

The Role of the Vagus Nerve: Relaxing Up

As Fear and I had more space between us, things were going on in my nervous system and physiology that are worth mentioning.

The vagus nerve is the very cabling that sends messages of safety between body and mind.

The vagus branches down in two pathways, emerging from the left and right side of the brain stem, running down each side of the neck into the pelvis, communicating with almost every organ along the way. But like a tree that grows roots down into the earth to bring essential nutrients back up, the vagus extends down into the body to bring essential messages back up to the brain. In fact, 80 percent of the vagus fibers *flow upwards,* while only 20 percent flow from brain to body.

It is through the vagus nerve that our brain knows what is currently happening in our body—the condition of our organs, our gut, and all our physiological systems, as well as our feelings, and, most importantly, *how we feel about our feelings*. The vagus nerve delivers the news that it is safe to shift into relaxation.

Our ability to calm our mind is truly a bottom-up process. Understanding this is a game changer.

As we already discussed, the vagus passes through the opening in the diaphragm. When the diaphragm moves fully and rhythmically, the vagus receives the stimulation (and the hormones) it needs to initiate calm. But when we are tense, it restricts diaphragmatic movement, which minimizes vagus stimulation.

As you can see, intentionally releasing overall tension supports more diaphragm movement and, therefore, fuller breath. This, in turn, sends stronger signals up to the brain that we are safe.

Walking with Fear

That day with Willow, after calming myself and creating some space between my impatience and her fear, I was finally able to say, "Sweetheart, I know you're feeling scared. Going upstairs is really hard for you, isn't it?"

"So scary," she said, her voice firm.

"And I know you really want to get Barbie's perfect dress for the day," I added.

"Barbie needs the pink one today. The one with the white polka dots," she said.

"I have an idea," I told her gently. "Let's all go together—you, me, and your fear."

Willow looked at me, confused.

"I'll hold your hand," I continued, "and we'll walk together. We can bring your fear along with us. It's okay to let it be here."

"Walk with my fear?" she asked, hesitating.

"Yes, we can feel our feet on the ground, and take a deep breath, and say hello to fear," I said, and then we began, "Hello, Fear. I know you're here."

Willow repeated after me, "Hello, Fear. I know you're here."

"Fear, I know you just want to keep me safe. Thank you," I said softly.

"Fear, I know you just want me to be safe. Thank you," Willow echoed.

"But I'm okay now. I'm safe," I reassured her.

"I'm okay now. I'm safe," she said quietly.

"And you can come with us if you want," I added.

"You can come with us if you want," she repeated.

We kept repeating these phrases as we walked hand in hand.

Willow's tight, white-knuckled grip softened, her hand warm in mine. Her breath became calm and steady. And instead of rushing to get Barbie's things, she slowed down, easing into a more relaxed pace.

Unbeknownst to her five-year-old self, Willow had developed an emotional pattern, unintentionally reinforcing it each time she tried to avoid the discomfort of leaving the safety of mom to venture out and get what she wanted.

Willow had no idea this was happening inside her—and most of us don't realize that how we react to difficult moments reinforces our emotional patterns, strengthening our tension. But this is the very wiring we can change through Pausing.

Our Tension Becomes a Habit

The reason it's so essential to understand tension and how to respond to it is that it is not only present when we are nervous about flying or Barbie outfits. We all carry habitual tension all day, every day, for all of our lives.

Whenever I teach a yoga class, especially to beginners, and I instruct them to "drop your shoulders" or "unclench your jaw," I can see my students' bodies soften. Invariably, many of the students share afterward that they were certain I was referring to their specific body. Most people are completely unaware—not only that they're almost always tensing up, but that everyone else is, too. Our habitual tensing—clenching our jaws, hunching our shoulders, tightening our bellies, holding our breath—gradually turns into chronic tension. We may carry tension patterns from the past year, the last decade, or even our entire lives. Our tension patterns might not be our own but inherited from our parents, grandparents, and lineage. Yet, in most situations, these habits aren't necessary or helpful. Clenching our jaws or hiking up our shoulders rarely improves the moment. Instead, they are unnecessary "add-ons" to the required physical actions. It's not usually helpful to grip our bellies or hold our breath. Most often, it's the opposite.

Our chronic habitual tension will keep us stuck in the stress response loop. Our tension leaves us feeling more defensive or aggressive because the underlying reason it is there in the first place is the need to protect ourselves. Consciously or unconsciously, when we feel tense we feel discomfort, pain, irritability, or agitation. It limits our ability for clarity and intentional choices, and prevents us from feeling a sense of safety, ease, and connection.

We release our tension, not by forcing it to change—not by stretching it or demanding it let go—but rather by supporting ourselves.

When we begin with creating a foundation of support, sending a message of safety through grounding and messages for calming through breathing, we can then turn our attention to the tension we hold, and we can purposely stop gripping, squeezing, and holding on for dear life.

When talking about Relaxing on purpose, we are referring to the obvious, unnecessary, habitual tension responses we can learn to recognize. As we get familiar with our habits, we know the areas to return to and stop energizing. To stop "adding on." When we Relax on purpose—dropping our shoulders, unclenching our jaw—it signals to the rest of the body that we can ease up. This, in turn, sends a message to the brain to calm down, let down its guard, and relax even more.

Titrating: One Step at a Time

For a couple of weeks, Willow and I did this little ritual, holding hands and talking with Fear as we would go to another floor in the house.

Somewhere along the way, I would look up from my work and see Willow going by herself into the next room—without asking for support. She'd return and tell me, "Mommy, I got Barbie new shoes."

I said. "Great job! Let me see Barbie's new look."

Then, there was the day I saw her out of the corner of my eye standing at the foot of the stairs. I could see she was hesitant to take that first step. But she made it all the way up and back down (very quickly, of course).

"Wow! Did you just go upstairs by yourself?!" I asked.

"I did!" she said with pride.

In those first solo ventures, she raced like a sprinter, talking to Fear the whole way. But slowly, something shifted. Over time, she stopped rushing and started walking; her movements relaxed as if she'd forgotten she was ever afraid. Watching her navigate the house so freely, it was hard to believe there was once a time when she couldn't. Willow took these steps, a little bit at a time . . . She learned to go upstairs in stages. First with me. Then, to the room next to us. Then, the room on the other side of the house. Then upstairs. One step at a time. Coming back each time to reconnect with support—in this case, the safety of me.

This is titrating.

When we titrate, we expose ourselves to something new, a little bit at a time. This method allows us to learn and integrate this newness gradually. We are building a foundation upon which we can grow.

Small Steps, Big Change

One of my long-standing mottoes has been "a little + often = a lot." This truth was scientifically reinforced for me when Willow was young and dealing with her life-threatening, anaphylactic gluten allergy. Her allergy was so severe that if I ate a bagel and then kissed her on the lips, it could stop her from breathing.

At ten years old, Willow was admitted to the world's first oral immunology clinical trial study on wheat gluten. This study had her ingesting a little wheat protein (gluten) powder daily. Her dose was increased by a few milligrams every two weeks for three years. Over the three years, she progressively notched up from her starting point of six milligrams of gluten—the threshold she could handle before full-blown anaphylaxis—until her immune system could digest gluten rather than think it was the enemy.

For context, *one large piece* of wheat bread contains approximately 4,443 milligrams of gluten—almost 750 times what she could initially ingest.

Over these three years, titrating one milligram at a time, Willow's system learned to tolerate a piece of bread. And eventually, even a whole pizza, should she wish.

This is what we are doing when we titrate. We are expanding our capacity to be with challenging stimuli little by little. (Just to be clear, we're not referring to enduring abuse, staying in unsafe situations, or any circumstances where we need to defend and protect ourselves from acute danger.)

The takeaway is that to truly integrate changes, it is essential to work so that our body and mind can tolerate our conditions—so the nervous system does not get alarmed. An armored-up nervous system cannot easily make changes.

Each time we are able to modulate and down-regulate our nervous system on purpose, we grow our capacity to do it again. Little by little, we can increase our tolerance for our conditions, as Willow did with her immune system test. This is what Willow did while moving from room to room as well.

When we can stay grounded (Land), breathe (Arrive), and intentionally Relax while gradually exposing ourselves to our "challenge"—whether it's something within our bodies or a situation in our lives—our nervous system receives a signal of safety. This allows us to engage with the present moment in a new, more empowered way.

This whole process of titrating *depends on* a sense of safety but *also* requires a friendly attitude. In fact, it's actually our welcoming attitude that creates the sense of safety we need to Relax. It is a prerequisite to relaxation. And we practice this a little bit at a time. Again and again.

The first step is becoming aware of our habitual, unnecessary tension. What's on your checklist? Start with two or three areas. For me, it's my jaw (I'm always clenching), and my shoulders (I'm always tensing them up), and my hands (I curl up into fists).

The second step is to develop a new relationship to these tensing habits and develop the new neurological wiring of being able to Relax on purpose. This step takes a little practice. Because releasing our tension requires a warmth toward ourselves that many of us are not used to, most often, when we find something in our bodies that is uncomfortable, or that we want to change, or that we don't like, we tend to judge ourselves, bully ourselves, berate, punish, and force ourselves, insist things change.

But when it comes to tension (and most things, according to neuroscience), trying to force it away will only make it, well, more tense.

We need to learn to hold our own hand and take tiny steps toward our uncomfortable feelings so that, incrementally, we feel safe enough to relax.

Notice how you are holding yourself. Notice any gripping or clenching you might be doing, even though you don't need to be doing it. This is habitual tension.

Circumstances Do Not Need to Be "Relaxing"

Many of us think we can only relax on a yoga mat, in a calm room with candles and soothing music, or while on retreat—only to tense back up the moment we turn our phone on, check the news, step into the "real world," or spend time with family. Relaxing is not about our circumstances.

We don't need to be on vacation, light incense, rub oil, or dim the lights to relax. While those things can certainly help, what we're really practicing is building a supportive relationship with ourselves and our experience, no matter where we are.

Rather than trying to take away challenging circumstances, we are changing our inner conditions to work with whatever is present.

When I teach this concept to my students, I ask them if they remember playing with a snow globe. I say: Imagine shaking the globe and seeing all the glittery snowflakes swirl around; imagine that all that glitter represents everything going on in your life—the good and the bad.

Often, when we think of relaxation, we think of it as possible only when the swirling snow has finally subsided.

The truth is, even when the snowflakes settle, we know it won't last for long. Perfect conditions don't exist, and before we know it, another swirling storm will emerge again.

Relaxing—releasing our tension—is more an act of creating space for what is there, not trying to make it go away. It doesn't necessarily mean we will feel "good" or even "happy." (Sorry.) We are learning that we can be *with the swirling* without always needing to wait for the snow to settle completely *and* without needing *perfect* conditions, whether our snow is the swirling weather around us or the swirling weather within us.

We do this by practicing Relaxing with *whatever* swirls are happening in the present moment.

We're learning not to add more tension to what we already feel—not to pile more stress on top of our existing stress. It's all about training ourselves, not to add on. When we Relax on purpose, we create space in our bodies, allowing us to widen our attention and expand our awareness of the present moment. As we Relax on purpose, we can be with the snowflakes and the conditions of the storm.

Learning to Relax is learning to BE with tension.

We are practicing Relaxing—softening (even just a tiny bit)—when we have the impulse to harden. We're practicing relaxing and opening when we feel the impulse to do the opposite.

We are learning to Relax so we can be more open and compassionate in the daily moments of our lives.

The attitude with which we meet our tense muscles matters. Relaxation only happens when we feel safe.

Lightening Up

Have you ever heard of hand-washing training? You use a special gel soap, wash your hands, then put your hands under an ultraviolet lamp and it illuminates the areas you missed. It shows you where you still have germs lingering. This helps you learn the areas that you might unconsciously miss while you wash, so you can clean hands more thoroughly.

We do something similar in conscious relaxation. As we get more familiar with our unnecessary tension habits, we can develop a new relationship with them. We can train ourselves to repeatedly release excess gripping and clenching and create more ease in our bodies.

Every day, we wash our hands. It's not like we wash once and we're then done for the week. In this same way, we continually have to "meet and release" our tension. Over and over again, several times a day. And the more we do it, the more quickly and easily we remember to do it again.

We are learning how to identify and release habitual unnecessary tension in the body, and eventually in the mind. We are learning to grow more aware of those often-overlooked spots, the unconscious ones we've gotten used to bypassing. Once we find these hidden tensions, we can return to them more easily to release them more quickly.

It's easier to release our tension when we know our go-to areas. Since at any time of day I can check in and find that I am squinting my eyes, clenching my jaw, or hiking up my shoulders, I return to these areas, on purpose, several times a day. When I consciously ease my three habitual areas, it sends a message to the rest of my body to relax more.

Just Noticing: A Pre-Practice Inquiry

Before you Pause to Relax, it's helpful to identify any areas of your body where you may be holding tension. So we will begin with a brief body scan. Remember to scan through your body with kindness. Be gentle with what you find. We are learning to notice when, how, and where we tense up, and rather than judging what we find, or berating ourselves, we are practicing being gentle with ourselves. We are simply noticing how things are.

Let's begin:

- Bring your awareness to the area of your eyes. Are you squinting your eyes? Or tensing any of the muscles around your brows and temples?
- Bring your awareness to the area of your jaw. Are you clenching your jaw? Pursing your lips? Tensing your tongue?
- Bring your awareness to your shoulders and arms. Are you hiking up your shoulders? Tightening your arms? Making fists?
- Bring your awareness to your abdomen. Are you gripping anywhere in your abdomen? Are you holding your breath or resisting your breath in some way?
- Bring your awareness to your seat and legs. Are you squeezing your seat? Tightening your thighs? Curling your toes?

Consider three areas where tension feels the most obvious, tangible, accessible. Areas that might, at any given time, be tense without your conscious control. These are areas you can return to every time you Pause.

PAUSE TO PRACTICE RELAXING

In the practice, on each exhale, we are simply, kindly, allowing ourselves to release any unnecessary work, effort, clenching. I'll use my personal three go-to areas of tension as examples; however, you'll want to work with the areas most pertinent to you—consider three areas you discovered in the Pre-Practice Inquiry. You may sit, stand, or even lie down when practicing Relaxing.

- To begin, notice where you meet support: the ground, a chair, a couch. Let your body rest; Land on the ground. Allow your mind to Arrive on your breath; feel your breath flowing through you.
- On your next inhale, notice your jaw. As you exhale, allow your jaw to release; to dangle from the back of your ears. Jaw unhinged. Jaw soft. Allow your whole mouth to soften, your tongue to widen and rest on the floor of your mouth.
- On your next inhale, notice your shoulders. As you exhale, allow your shoulders to fall from your ears, your shoulder blades slide down your back. Shoulders rest on your body. Effortless arms.
- On your next inhale, notice your hands. As you exhale, let your hands unfurl, fingers soft. Sense the volume inside your palms. Spacious hands. Open hands.

Again.

- On your next exhale, your jaw dangles.
- On your next exhale, shoulders drop.
- On your next exhale, hands soften.
- On one last *long* exhale, allow your jaw to unhinge, shoulders to drop, fists to unfurl. Let yourself Relax, *just as you are.* Here. Now.

To close, stay aware of your body on the ground, your breath flowing through you, re-relaxing your jaw, shoulders, hands—while you expand your awareness into the space around you. Set an intention to continually re-relax through your day.

May you Relax and welcome yourself
here, now,
just as you are.

CHAPTER 6

Land, Arrive, Relax: Integrating the First LAR

THE FIRST LAR changes everything. It is the gift of self-regulation that allows us to reenter the present moment with more resources and the ability to stay connected to ourselves so that we can open more curiously and compassionately to ourselves and others. It's the difference between reacting from a place of stress and responding with awareness in the moment.

Upstairs, Downstairs

When I was upstairs in my bathroom, after I stormed away from my mother and Willow at the table, after I slammed the bathroom door, my whole body hot with anger, I could feel that my shoulders were hiked up. High.

I've been aware of my shoulders being up with tension and have been practicing releasing them for thirty years. And, still, at any given time when I check in, and my shoulders are up, I may still slip into the old habit of berating myself for it. "I can't believe I can't stop hiking up my shoulders. I'll never learn to relax. What's wrong with me?"

As I heard this voice in my head for maybe the millionth time, I chose to receive it differently—not as criticism, but as an invitation to soften.

Land. Arrive. Relax.

I paid attention to my next three breaths.

I felt my feet on the ground, my body Landing on support.

I felt my breath Arrive in my body.

I Relaxed my jaw, shoulders, and fists.

Three breaths later, I felt more connected to myself. My head was not going to pop off. But my emotions were still overwhelming me.

Exhaling, I felt my feet Land on the ground.

Inhaling, I felt my breath Arrive in my body.

Exhaling, I Relaxed my jaw, shoulders, and fists.

Three more breaths later, I felt more connected to myself. I could see how I felt ashamed of being unable to control how my daughter spoke to my mother five minutes ago. I could also see how funny it was that I thought I was in control of anyone. But I still needed more calm.

Another breath, I felt my feet Land on the ground, again.

Another breath, I felt my breath Arrive in my body, again.

Another breath, I Relaxed my jaw, shoulders, and fists, again.

And I then softened. I softened toward myself: *What a hard moment for you*, I thought.

And then, I felt a softening toward Willow and my mom. *What a hard moment this was for us all.*

I put my hand on my heart. *It made sense that you got overwhelmed*, I said to myself silently.

I softened toward myself again, with a gesture of forgiveness for exploding. I wasn't proud of my reactions. But I also understood that several old stories, habitual patterns, were at play in my body and my mind.

I let myself truly feel my hand on my heart. The forgiving gesture of my compassionate hand softened me further. I now felt calm and wanted to repair things.

So, one more time for good measure:

Exhaling, I felt my feet Land on the ground.

Inhaling, I felt my breath Arrive in my body.

Exhaling, I Relaxed my jaw, shoulders, and fists.

Then, I went downstairs . . .

Brain Shift

This first LAR initiates the Pause—a breath between stimulus and response, a moment where choice becomes possible.

The first LAR is the process of *conscious* relaxation, which I refer to as Relaxing on purpose. This first LAR is how we turn on our relaxation response. The more relaxed we are, the more we turn on the part of our brain that can mindfully Listen and consciously choose our response—the goal of the second LAR.

As we Land, Arrive, and Relax—again and again—we are rewiring our nervous system. Through this first LAR, we begin to be more conscious of how we resist feeling support underneath us, minimizing our breath, and tensing our bodies.

Eventually, this is the same process that helps us identify our habitual patterns of thinking and behaving, our emotional looping, and our "unconscious" conditioning. We begin by working with our tension, because when the body is more relaxed, it sends messages to the brain to shift and expand awareness.

Each time we can Pause and consciously Relax, we may find deeper tensions in our body and mind that we can work with. Or we may notice something in the "swirl" that we haven't spent time examining before.

We may realize that we are living life as a series of automatic reactions to what is happening around us. We begin to notice the old stories we carry, looping through negative thinking patterns (as we'll explore shortly). We become aware of our pain, suffering, and the deep desire to find relief.

Pausing prepares us to Relax *with* the circumstances of life. We are learning to stay open to daily tensions without exaggerating, avoiding, exacerbating, or resisting them. Without reacting to everything from the filter of our stress response—a stance of aggression (fight), avoidance (flight), or withdrawal (freeze), the categories of behavior we are stuck in when we feel threatened.

We will never be able to control how someone else thinks or behaves. We will never be able to control many of the events around us. These are facts I repeatedly remind myself of. I realize that many of the things that trigger me in my life will never go away. But my relationship to these things *can* change.

We can improve our chances of becoming more familiar with what we bring to each situation. We can better understand the way we guard, defend, and protect ourselves and how this creates our tension. We can come to know the "stories" we hold under our tension. And the more we understand ourselves and attend to ourselves, the more we can increase the odds that we won't be as habitually reactive to ourselves or the world around us. This takes dedication, discipline, and practice.

We practice Pausing on purpose, all day long, so that we can meet our "stress" differently in the tougher moments of our lives.

Our habits, even the ones we don't like, are borne out of routine. Repeated actions develop deep neural pathways for the brain to send instructions, which ensures repeat behaviors. These pathways are like well-trodden paths that have emerged in a dense forest because they have been walked on over and over again. They are the "easiest" routes to take.

We have gotten so used to our usual routes that we don't even consider the idea that we have other choices.

If we are going to interrupt previous well-established reactions, routines, and habits, we need to do it on purpose. Which means we need discipline to do something different.

Our ability to choose our response is available once we set a foundation through Pausing. As we calm ourselves, we activate the prefrontal cortex, the part of the brain that allows our awareness to expand.

If all you take from this book is this first LAR, it will be life-changing.

We Pause to create space to be with the current moment as it is, in a more spacious and open way.

Repeat, Repeat, Repeat

Let me share a little secret. Many people consider me a "professional relaxer." I assure you, this is not because I am *naturally* relaxed. Or even because I'm *often* relaxed. Rather, it's because I am really good at *re-relaxing.*

I practice re-relaxing again and again. I've been Pausing all day long to re-relax for decades. Relaxation isn't my default setting—it's my chosen practice.

Our goal is not to "stay relaxed," but to continually come back to a more regulated state.

Conscious relaxation is not something we do just once. It is something we do continually—consciously—over and over again.

We are practicing meeting ourselves and the present moment in a new way—free from the filter of chronic stress, habitual defenses, or past wounds. While Pausing is the practice and the discipline of interrupting our habitual reactions and creating space for reconnecting to ourselves, it is also the foundation we need to feel safe and calm enough to come home into our bodies. Just as we are. Here, in the present moment.

We practice Pausing so we can increase our ability—physically, mentally, emotionally, and relationally—to respond calmly, clearly, and wisely.

We rewrite our relationship with stress each time we meet the present moment with curiosity. This brings us to the second LAR, which will build on everything we've explored so far, deepening the practice of self-compassion and awareness.

If the first LAR brings us into the present moment, the second LAR is about how we can embody ourselves *to be with* the present.

In the second LAR we learn how we can Listen and Attend to ourselves, so that we can better Respond to what we find happening in the present moment.

Let your body Land on the ground.

Let your breath Arrive in your body.

Allow yourself to Relax, whatever can relax, a little bit more.

90-SECOND PAUSE PRACTICE TO RESET YOUR NERVOUS SYSTEM: LAND, ARRIVE, AND RELAX

This 90-second practice brings you through the first LAR three times. However, when you incorporate this practice during your day and do it on the spot, you may find that one round of three breaths—or even a single breath practice—can still be a profound Pause. I encourage you to practice this first LAR Pause for three breaths before each meal, before you answer a text or pick up a call, or even during a conversation. The more regularly you practice this first LAR, the more quickly you will be able to reset your nervous system and your presence when you need it most.

- On an inhale, bring your awareness to where you meet support. As you exhale, allow all your weight to drain down and rest on the ground. Let yourself Land.
- On the next inhale, feel your breath Arrive in your body. Let your mind Arrive on the flow of your breath. As you exhale, follow the breath back out into the space around you. Let yourself Arrive on the breath. Here. Now.
- On the next inhale, become aware of your jaw, shoulders, hands. As you exhale, let your jaw dangle, shoulders drop, fists unfurl. Let yourself Relax more.

Again . . .

- Inhaling, *feel* support under your body. Exhaling, let yourself Land on the ground, again.
- Inhaling, feel the breath Arriving in your body. Exhaling, let your mind rest on your breath as it flows out.
- Inhaling, allow the breath to soften you inside. Exhaling, jaw softens, shoulders drop, fists unfurl. Relax, just as you are. Here. Now.

Three more complete breaths:

- Feel your body Land on the ground.
- Allow your mind to Arrive on your breath.
- Relax your jaw, shoulders, hands.

To close, take one more complete breath to simultaneously Land, Arrive, and Relax. Stay aware of your body on the ground, your breath flowing, re-relaxing your jaw, shoulders, hands—while you expand your awareness into the space around you. Set an intention to Pause for three breaths—Land, Arrive, and Relax—repeatedly throughout your day.

Land, Arrive, Relax.
May you Pause,
grow grounded,
and expand into the spaciousness
that is always here for you.

CHAPTER 7

Listen

It was 2010. I had been teaching yoga and meditation for over a decade and was eighteen years into a regular practice. Sitting on my yoga mat on the teaching platform, I had just closed the last class of a five-day retreat.

Grounded, breathing deeply, I felt present, connected, and content. The group began getting ready to leave, rolling their mats, gathering belongings, and sharing good-byes. Several students approached me at the front of the room for a more personal, one-on-one good-bye, some even offering heartfelt insights about their experience.

I was happy to see Dan waiting to chat with me. It was his first yoga retreat. His wife had dragged him to my program, and I wasn't quite sure how he was feeling because he kept an adept poker face.

Standing confidently, he admitted, "I really didn't know if I'd make it through this week."

I expected him to share something I hear a lot, like, ". . . because the yoga was harder than I thought," or ". . . because my mind was all over the place," or ". . . because I didn't realize how much emotion I was holding," or ". . . because a lot of difficult things surfaced." I was prepared to respond empathetically and offer encouragement through his struggle.

Instead, he continued, "At the beginning of the program, I thought I should leave. I didn't know how I would get through it, because I HATE your voice."

Did I hear him right?

"*My voice?*" I asked, a little stunned.

"Yes. I can't stand the sound of your voice," he said, unapologetically.

For a moment, it was like an out-of-body experience. *Does he realize he just insulted me?*

Honestly, I never thought of my voice as something people liked or disliked until 2002, when I released my guided relaxation CD, *Relaxmore.* Since then, I regularly get emails from strangers all over the world about how much they "*love* my voice" and how soothing, grounding, and comforting they find it. Many people have told me that they even put my meditations on as background sound while doing other things to stay calmed by my voice.

So naturally, my voice became something I thought of as an asset, a part of me that others find *likable.* I admit this gave me confidence and even pride, feelings that didn't come easily. I might even say, my voice became part of my identity. I was *Jillian with the great voice.*

Dan's words felt personal—like an attack on my worth, my value—on *me.* And my habitual response would be to recoil in shame. At one time, I would have slid into the habit of thinking that I was not good enough and should work harder to be better. That if I got *his* approval, it would make me a better teacher—a better person. And, if I didn't go in that direction, I would have at least thought of him as a jerk. A bully. A total dick.

But this time I did something different.

I Paused.

I could feel the thick, folded yoga blanket under my seat, and how the solid wood stage completely supported my body. I felt my breath filling my chest while I consciously dropped my shoulders, just what I needed to stay grounded and open in that moment.

And the most amazing thing happened next. I was able to stay in the conversation. And I *wanted* to understand more.

"What specifically bothers you about my voice?" I asked, wondering if it might be my New Jersey accent.

Without hesitation, he responded, "Everything."

He was silent for a moment, though it felt like a long time, and then continued, "I hate the sound of your voice, your pacing. The way you use inflections. All of it. Which is why I was so surprised that I started to actually appreciate what you were saying."

Listening to him, I could hear the sound of my own breath as I exhaled. I noticed I was still present, Listening, aware that I *should* be contracting into myself, but wasn't.

He continued, "After a couple of days, despite not liking your voice, I heard so many things I needed to hear that I really started to tune in to what you were saying. So, I kind of got over not liking your voice. I want to thank you. This week wound up being really powerful for me."

It is true that I initially heard Dan's comment as an insult. But once I Landed, Arrived, and Relaxed, I was able to Listen—and it no longer felt like an attack.

I didn't sweat. I didn't shrink or harden. My vision didn't blur. I did not get lost in an echo chamber of "I hate your voice . . . I hate your voice . . . I hate your voice . . ."

I didn't feel shame or anger or scramble to find a way to get his approval. I did not experience any of the habitual things that happen when I feel rejected, diminished, or not good enough. Instead, I just continued Listening.

The Ability to Listen

We are learning to Pause so we can Listen without the filter of our habitual protective mechanisms—so that rather than being hijacked by our reactive tendency to become defensive, shut down, or make assumptions about what is being said, we are better able to meet whatever arises with curiosity. We are better able to choose our Response. This requires us to practice regulating our nervous system *as* we are listening. Which means we need to be aware not only of what we are "taking in" from others, but also of what is happening within ourselves as we are listening.

If we can know what is happening inside of our bodies, our emotions, our tensing, our habitual ways of shutting down, while we are listening, then we can choose to relax and open on purpose to whomever we are listening. We can better understand what they are actually saying, rather than interpreting their meaning through the filter of our own stress.

Returning to our snow globe metaphor from Chapter 5, we can envision the snow globe as not only representing our relationship to *outer* circumstances, but also serving as a metaphor for our *inner* life. Picture the swirling glitter snow as our thoughts, emotions, and bodily sensations—constantly shifting and in motion. This swirling reflects the brain's default activity: a continuous hum of assessment, analysis, and memory. In fact, brain imaging shows that neurological activity persists even when we aren't consciously thinking, such as dreaming during sleep. The brain's natural state is fundamentally restless.

Just like with our external environment, we often think of inner calm as the moment when the snow settles and the globe becomes clear—when all the swirling inside our mind ceases. But in reality, some amount of inner activity will *always* be present. If our mind is like this snow globe, then even when we feel *initially* calm, Pausing and tuning in often reveals the difficult emotions and sensations we carry in our bodies and minds. The snow might have settled, but it's not gone entirely.

When we truly open ourselves to both our inner and outer environments—especially after spending much of our lives not paying that kind of attention—we begin noticing far more than we're used to. Initially, this heightened awareness can feel overwhelming.

So, it's worth not only noting *what* we find swirling, but *how* we pay attention to the swirl.

When I teach the snow globe metaphor I actually hold up a real snow globe. I ask my students to notice the clear globe, the glass sphere, the spacious container that the glitter swirls within. Then, I invite them to visualize:

You are the snow *globe.*

You are *not* the snow.

Your thoughts, emotions, and sensations are the snowflakes. Swirling is the nature of snow.

You are the *container.*

And you are the *space.*

So rather than being caught up in the swirl, where we are habitually reacting from our feelings or our tension, we practice relaxing with whatever swirling is happening at the moment. We practice being present with whatever we find inside our bodies and minds. We shift our attention to include the space of the globe—our *spaciousness*—rather than hyper-focusing *only* on the snow.

We Land on the ground.

We allow our breath to Arrive in our body and our mind to Arrive on our breath, in the present.

We Relax our tension, on purpose.

These first three steps are how we Pause in the face of whatever is happening in front of us and within us, enabling us to widen our attention and Listen more openly to *all* the present moment conditions. This moment of Pause allows us, despite our ongoing background and foreground noise, to understand more clearly what may need our attention and how we wish to participate in this present moment.

Listening in this way is a mindful practice—an awareness of what is happening inside and around us—and choosing to open anyway, moment by moment.

Deep Listening

This conscious act of mindfully Listening, which includes the intent to be open, to understand, and to learn, all with an attitude of kindness, is often called Deep Listening.

Deep Listening is only available once we set a foundation through Pausing. As we calm ourselves, we activate the prefrontal cortex, allowing our awareness to expand. In this way, Pausing will enable us to remain centered, helping us feel a sense of connection and safety. Centeredness changes how we respond. It helps us manage our stress and triggers, allowing us to stay more open and curious neurologically and more available for Deep Listening.

This way of Listening allows us to stay attuned to what's happening within ourselves as we engage with the world around us. In other words, while Listening outwardly—to others and the environment—we remain aware of our feelings, our reactions, and our emotions. As we engage in Deep Listening, we gain a *clearer perspective* on this inner swirl.

Yes, a lot is going on here. It's like we are practicing both precision and broadening our awareness at the same time. Focus and concentration *and* expanding our view.

While this may sound complicated, most of us already do it in our everyday lives. For example, driving a car requires focus and concentration to steer, accelerate, brake, and follow directions. At the same time, it demands open awareness of the ever-changing environment. We are continually oscillating between these two states. We can be driving skillfully and also can appreciate the joy of seeing kids play soccer on the lawn, yet instantly react when their ball rolls out into the street.

While Listening is a receptive practice, it also takes some skill to bring our attention to the present—to take in what we *hear* and discern what we are paying attention to.

Through practice, we can cultivate skills that allow us to get better—and even very good—at Listening. That will enable us to develop the ability to shift back and forth between attention to our outer circumstances and what's happening within us, and take in an ever-widening breadth of information—just like when we're driving.

When I paused to talk with Dan at the end of my workshop, I experienced this broadened awareness. Again, I initially heard Dan's comment as offensive. But once I Landed, Arrived, and Relaxed, and was able to Listen, it no longer *felt* like an *affront*. It was almost like I was watching a movie, I could see and hear the whole scene—what was going on in the entire picture frame. Rather than zooming in and creating a very narrow and tight experience inside me, I had a wide-lens view of the bigger story. I was not trapped inside the character this was happening to.

I could fully sense myself: I could Listen to what was being said, while I could also feel my own body and feelings. I could take in the *content* of what Dan was saying without disconnecting from myself. I was more physically comfortable and more mentally clear, which allowed me to consider what he was really sharing:

I came in with a lot of resistance. I feel so different now. This helped me. I am happy I came and stayed. Thank you.

Negativity Bias

The reason we need to develop a broad, conscious awareness when we are Listening is that by nature, rather than seeing things *as they are*, we are hardwired to continually look for and prepare for danger. Neuroscientists refer to this as the negativity bias. We all have it because it keeps us safe.

The negativity bias is our tendency to readily register negative experiences, thoughts, and feelings and dwell on these events. According to the National Science Foundation, 95 percent of our thoughts are repeated thoughts, and 80 percent of these repeated thoughts are negative.

It is not only adverse *events* we tend to dwell on. We also tend to dwell on how we feel about the events and ourselves. We dwell on how we feel inadequate, ashamed, hurt, or powerless, and how we need to improve and do more.

We are wired to dwell on the belief that we are "not enough."

I relate so completely to this research. I am always wondering, *Did I just do a good job (on whatever thing I just did)?* I am literally asking myself this question all day long—even after writing that last sentence. What is good enough? And while awareness of this habit was a big revelation to me, the bigger revelation was realizing that my knee-jerk, 80-percent-of-the-time answer is, *No, it's not good enough.*

Let me share a little story about this. I recently taught a ninety-person retreat that went phenomenally well. The feedback was incredible. It felt so affirming to me to have my work so well received. An hour after arriving home, still glowing from the weekend, I received an email review from a student who attended another one of my programs a few months earlier, saying that it was not what they had expected and that they were disappointed. Instantly, my delight from ninety rave reviews plummeted as a result of this one person's experience.

I have grown to know this "negativity bias" habit of mine, so I was able to observe it happening. Taking a moment to Pause helped me not get sucked into an old pattern where I would have ruminated on this for days, if not weeks. For a second, I could even laugh at myself.

Traveling in the Snow (with Mirrors)

As you might imagine, our constant interior chastising of ourselves is just kicking up more and more snow inside our globe. We experience this as feelings of low-level—or high-level—anxiety, sometimes so deeply that we are not even consciously aware of it. But we don't have to be controlled by our well-designed nervous system in this way.

Remember my Thanksgiving outburst—a huge mental snowstorm. Inside my mind, I was raging at my daughter for being so insensitive and worrying that my mother's feelings were hurt. I was also feeling like I failed to protect my mother and raise a polite child. I must be a shitty mom and a shitty daughter or none of us would be in this situation right now. Oh, and I'm definitely a fraud of a teacher. Because I just freaked out and left the table—*and* my shoulders were still tense.

I felt angry. Hurt. Inadequate. Disappointed. Ashamed. I was overwhelmed inside this big swirl of emotions.

But *also*, I could see my emotions clearly and even name them once I took a breath and felt my feet on the ground. And another breath to notice the air arriving in my body. And another breath to unclench my jaw and let my shoulders relax. I could Listen to them, and choose to respond from there, when I was ready.

We will learn more about working with challenging conditions in the next chapter, but for now, let's simply acknowledge the fact that we are not just standing still all day in our snow globe. We are moving through our lives. Our goal with this work is not to change the weather. We won't always have control over the conditions of the roads we travel on. In this sense, we don't have to *change* anything. In fact, we simply have to know what the conditions are—and practice not getting pulled off the road by it all.

This way, we can drive confidently and responsively and choose how to relate to our conditions. Sometimes that requires decisive action, and sometimes it requires pausing and opening more. We are setting internal conditions to be able to make moment-to-moment decisions about how we will relate and respond rather than constantly reacting from a place of stress.

When we grow more grounded, present, and relaxed, we begin to see more clearly what we are carrying—and this can be uncomfortable.

From my experience of working with thousands of people, I know that as soon as we check in to notice what's going on in the mind and body, we are likely to find unsettling things. We are likely to notice what is troublesome, painful, or distressing to us—in that moment, or maybe *for our lifetime.*

And yet, accessing all this information is ultimately to our greatest benefit.

Imagine driving a car without side and rearview mirrors. This would be very dangerous. The limited view would prevent us from taking into account the many factors around us (and within us), making us a hazard on the road to ourselves and everyone around us.

Deep Listening is the practice of allowing ourselves to have peripheral attention, open awareness, toward everything that is making up the present moment, while we also stay in our center. We are learning to stay grounded and be open, simultaneously.

We are learning to Listen in a way that leaves others feeling seen, heard, and understood. And we are learning to support ourselves in this way as well.

Listening in the Garden: Principles of the Practice

Equanimity is a central skill that is at the heart of Listening.

When I teach this on retreats, we begin with listening outwardly to nature. This is a friendly entry point. Not only because the sounds of nature are scientifically shown to further induce relaxation, but also because it's easy to be more neutral, open, curious, and welcoming to the natural soundscape.

Imagine sitting in a lush dense garden at the edge of a friendly forest. Imagine you are surrounded by flowers, all sorts of colorful vegetation, and trees. You would naturally hear a lot of different sounds. Birds singing, bees buzzing, small animals scurrying, wind moving through the trees. These would be natural sounds rising and falling in the garden.

When we sit in nature, we practice simply opening our awareness to the sounds around us. Since they are an organic aspect of nature, there is little, if any, impulse to reject the sounds or try to stop any of them from happening. There is little impulse to determine which ones "belong"—which are right or wrong. It's reasonable to simply allow the sounds to rise and fall in and out of your range of hearing, as they are happening—just noticing the ever-changing soundscape.

This is the fundamental aspect of a Listening practice—noticing, and allowing, what is happening in the present moment. This is equanimity. We might acknowledge sounds, but we refrain from judging them as good or bad. It is true we will be pulled more toward some sounds and less toward others. But we can notice that, too. So we simply rest, noticing what is happening in the present moment, through sound, as it is happening. Without expectation, but rather with curiosity and openness. Just opening to the symphony of nature.

Normally when we listen, say in a conversation or to ourselves—to what is going on in our bodies or minds—this is not the way we usually do it. Of course, in a garden or a forest it is "easy" to Listen like this.

However, I also teach Listening in this same way when I teach on Fifth Avenue in New York City, at lunch time during peak traffic, with ongoing street construction and sirens going by. This is where things get more complex. The soundscape is louder, and for many of us it can be more "intrusive" or agitating. But just because it can be a cacophony doesn't mean there are not pleasing sounds happening on Fifth Avenue as well.

While we will certainly hear the horns of traffic, construction, whistles blowing, and people shouting, we also hear people laughing, the hum of engaged conversations, music livening up the street, and we might also hear an occasional bird singing—even on Fifth Avenue.

No matter what the soundscape, it remains true that sounds will always rise and fall. Continually. No sound stays fixed forever. Just as a plane flies across the sky—it starts quiet, it gets louder, it gets quiet again, it disappears. Everything rises and falls. Even a jackhammer will eventually stop. Whatever sound you notice, any sound, just allow yourself to notice it.

When we are disturbed by what we hear, it's not only hard to hear what is also there that is pleasing, but it is also hard to not get caught up in our judgment about what we hear. We become disappointed, agitated, or angry at the things that are blowing up our peace. Or we become disappointed, agitated, or angry at ourselves that we can't block out the sounds, let alone welcome them.

Equanimity asks us to simply notice how things are—not only the *sound*, but also our *reaction* to the sound. This way we begin to understand there is a "trigger" and there is the way we "feel about the trigger." And if we can be open to both, we can create more room to notice what is actually happening.

When practicing, we can begin with the outer environment—the literal soundscape of the world around us. We Listen, taking in the sounds in close proximity and eventually the sounds from the more expansive environment, as a way of learning to allow sound to simply *be sound*, rising and falling in and out of our range of hearing.

The idea is to allow the sounds to rise and fall, both without trying to hone in on them and without trying to ignore them.

This is the skill that helps us welcome the "sounds" of our thoughts, feelings, and sensations when we begin to tune inward. To Listen to our inner garden, inner forest. Our inner city. And begin to open to what is present in us, with equanimity.

This is what we are practicing doing when we check in to see how we are—as we Listen inwardly. We are simply noticing the nature of what is present, inside the garden of ourselves.

You don't have to figure anything out or analyze your thoughts or feelings. You don't need to justify anything, diminish or exaggerate anything. You don't even need to stop the thoughts or feelings. You don't need to shut down the conversation. You are simply noticing all that rises and falls.

We are learning to notice what is happening. We might even notice that we like or dislike what is happening inside of us. But still, rather than adding on to what we notice, we are practicing just observing, and letting it all be.

The better we get at knowing what is happening inside of us while we are engaging with others, the more awareness we will have about the present moment, increasing our ability to work with our nervous system and set conditions to expand our capacity to choose our response.

The key in expanding our attention is to not *leave* ourselves while we are doing it. We are learning to open up our awareness, our Listening, our noticing, to take in the world—or what is in front of us in the moment—while we *also* remain aware of our bodies on the ground, in the spot where we are; as well as our breath flowing through us, and continuing to re-relax on purpose throughout the *whole* process.

PAUSE TO PRACTICE LISTENING

In this practice, we will set our foundation using the first LAR and then add on a few minutes of Listening. Try it for two to five minutes. Eventually, you may find that you can Listen deeply more quickly—and shorten the practice to even just a minute. But don't rush this step as you are learning it. Listening is where we begin to make more substantial changes in our lives. We're practicing allowing ourselves to expand to make space to notice what is happening in the present moment. We're learning to Listen outwardly to the world and to others—and we are learning to Listen to ourselves, to be with ourselves, with the way things are.

While practicing Listening, whatever you may feel or notice, just let it be. When you find you are having a "reaction" to anything you hear, simply notice that, too. Just notice yourself in a soft, welcoming way. Be gentle with yourself.

- To begin, bring your awareness to where your body meets support. As you exhale, allow all your weight to drain down and rest on the ground. Let yourself Land.
- On the next inhale, feel your breath Arrive in your body. As you exhale, follow the breath back out into the space around you. Let yourself Arrive on the breath. Here. Now.
- On the next inhale, become aware of your jaw, shoulders, hands. As you exhale, let your jaw dangle, shoulders drop, fists unfurl. Let yourself Relax more. Stay aware of your body on the ground, your breath flowing through you, re-relaxing while you expand your awareness into the space around you.

- Open up your hearing to notice the sounds around you. Allow yourself to Listen. Begin by noticing the sounds inside your room, maybe a fan, a creaking floor, a pet breathing nearby.
- Now, for a few breaths, expand your awareness to notice the sounds outside of your immediate space or room—maybe a TV in the next room, a dishwasher, people talking nearby. Then for a few breaths more, expand your awareness further—outside your home. You might hear birds, rain, or traffic. Whatever you notice, you might observe how no sound stays the same for very long. Allow all sounds to rise and fall without trying to hone in on them, without trying to ignore them.
- Begin to shift your attention toward the sound of your breath. Just like the sound around you, your breath will rise and fall. For the next few inhales and exhales, as you notice your breath flowing, expand your Listening to notice what is happening inside of you. Allow yourself to Listen to your inner landscape.
- As you notice any thoughts, emotions, and sensations, consider that, just like the soundscape around us, you don't have to block out anything. Gently allow yourself to Listen to what is here. Everything rises and falls, just as sound does around you. Just like sound and breath, thoughts and emotions and sensations, everything comes and goes.
- Stay gently centered while expanding your awareness, opening to take in more and more from the present moment, just as it is.

- Simply notice what you feel or hear inside. Tingling, heat, numbness. Busy mind. To-do list. Song lyrics. Sadness. Gratitude. Anxiety. Joy. Whatever you may feel or notice, just let it be. No judgment. Be soft with yourself as you are listening.

To close, you can place your hands on your body, maybe both on your chest, or one on your chest and one on your belly. Return you awareness to sense your seat on the ground, your body on the earth, your breath moving through your body. Relax the jaw, shoulders, hands. Allow your ears to open again to the sounds around you, your eyes to gently take in more of the space around you. Allow yourself to be present and open, and yet centered and grounded.

Set an intention to check back in again throughout the day to Pause for Listening, even if only for a minute.

May you Listen
to your body, mind, and heart.
May you Listen
outwardly to the world around you.
May you Listen,
simply Listen, to what is, just as it is.
Here, now.

CHAPTER 8

Attend

TARA BRACH, A psychologist and meditation teacher renowned for her work in mindfulness and self-compassion, once shared a story in a podcast on her website, tarabrach.com, about a man in a grocery store a few steps behind a mother with her toddler nestled in the front seat of her cart.

It went something like this: As the mom and toddler shopped in the first aisle, they passed the cookie section, and the child asked if they could have cookies. When the mother answered no, the little girl whined, "I want cookies."

The mother kept her cool and quietly responded, "Now, Ellen, we only have five aisles left. Don't be upset. It won't be long."

The man noted her composure.

A few minutes later, he passed the mother again in the candy aisle.

"Mommy, Mommy! Candy! I want candy."

"We are not buying candy today," the mother said.

The girl began to cry.

The mother gently and quietly answered again, "Now, now, Ellen, only two more aisles to go, and then we will be checking out."

The man was impressed.

He found himself behind them again, now at the checkout counter.

As they waited in line next to the gum display, the little girl tried to climb out of the cart to grab a pack of gum. The mother took a deep breath and guided her back into her seat. She calmly explained there would be no gum purchases, and the little girl burst into a tantrum.

The mother softly, patiently, said, "Now, now Ellen, we will be through this checkout stand in a few minutes, and then you can go home and have a nice nap."

The man stopped the mother just before she left and said, "I couldn't help but admire how patient you were with little Ellen."

The woman looked at him and smiled, "My little girl's name is Tammy. I'm Ellen."

Now, Now. I Wish I Had That Then

I wish I had heard this story of "Now, now Ellen" when Willow was a toddler, constantly asking me to go with her to another room to retrieve Barbie outfits. I would have used it a lot!

I am also 100 percent sure I would have used it every single morning when I had to get Willow out the door and to school on time. There were more mornings than not when I lost my cool, which left me frustrated at Willow and angry with myself. After wrangling her to get in the car, we'd pull up to school to the ring of the bell. "Now, now, Ellen" would have come in very handy on those days.

Instead, I'd feel exhausted and sad at the same time, wishing I could have been more patient. I'd apologize with a loving good-bye—but I'd still drive away feeling like a failure. And like a bad mom. And just overall bad.

In contrast, whenever my dear friend Nicole shared *her* parenting struggles with me, I'd listen caringly. I wouldn't even *have to try*. Organically, warm words of support would flow right from my heart. I'd confirm how hard parenting is and remind her of the many ways she is doing a great job and is such a good human.

I would always suggest she take a few moments to be kinder and more forgiving to herself. And maybe pre-plan for a more skillful response the next day.

Many of us treat our loved ones or good friends compassionately, but few have ever learned to treat ourselves this way, especially in times of vulnerability. When we are in pain, suffering, fearful, anxious, disappointed, or confused, we often habitually respond to ourselves in a way that escalates or solidifies these feelings—stimulating our stress response—rather than meeting ourselves supportively, kindly, and gently.

Attending to Ourselves: Self-Compassion

I remember a profound moment on a walk with another close friend, Jessica. It was an autumn morning; multicolored leaves covered the sidewalk and the air was just crisp enough to wear a hat and gloves. Feeling the push of the changing seasons, we were deep in conversation about our own need for change. She shared that she was shifting the way she was listening to herself. And just as importantly, talking to herself.

I asked her to tell me more.

"I was writing in my journal last week. I could not believe how harsh and judgmental I was toward myself. It's like I'm my own worst critic. I was re-reading it, and a lightbulb went off—something just clicked. I thought, *why do I believe these words?* They are simply not true. My friends would *never* speak to me this way; why is this the way I speak to myself?"

Most of us were never taught how to meet ourselves with compassion—the essential foundation for *being with* difficult emotions. Compassion is one of the conditions needed to regulate our nervous system, interrupt habitual reactions, and expand our behavioral options, empowering us to choose our response.

We use the first LAR to create a sense of safety and groundedness, a container to begin to get closer to our feelings and be with them. To pay attention to them—to Listen. And rather than avoiding them or adding more tension on top of our feelings—criticizing, judging, qualifying, or telling stories about them—we are simply practicing *being with what we feel* as we are feeling it and being with our shaky, queasy, uncomfortable, excitable sensations—with as much kindness and care as possible. Attending to ourselves as we experience it all.

To Attend to ourselves—and others—we start with the skill of Listening, and as you'll see, Listening and Attending work hand in hand.

How We Meet Ourselves

The way we meet ourselves will leave us feeling either like we have to harden, tense, and protect ourselves more or that we are supported, safe, and can soften and open.

Remember, our body listens to everything our mind says. Whenever we feel rejected, dismissed, diminished, or criticized by ourselves or others, our stress response activates instantly, often before we're even consciously aware.

We can learn self-compassion and create a change inside ourselves; we can change our nervous system and create new conditions in our body and mind. We can train to meet ourselves with an attitude of kindness. We can learn to Attend to ourselves. Ultimately, this supports us in changing how we meet conditions outside of ourselves.

Compassion as a Verb

I think about compassion as a verb. As something we do. And as something we can learn to do for ourselves. But how exactly do we do that?

Learning to offer ourselves compassion can feel more accessible when we understand these three science-backed techniques, all discussed in the following sections:

- Naming Your Inner Experience
- The 90-Second Rule
- Feeling Your Feelings

NAMING YOUR INNER EXPERIENCE: IDENTIFYING WHAT IS HAPPENING

When Willow and I walked upstairs together to get Barbie, we practiced saying "Fear is here," the mantra I created to help me when flying. We were naming how Willow felt: Afraid. Fearful. Anxious. Neuropsychologist Dr. Dan Siegel calls this technique "Name it to tame it." (This labeling practice is similar to the one used in Buddhist meditation, where, when you notice your thoughts and feelings distracting your attention, you simply note "thinking," and recenter your attention on your breath.)

Naming your experience is especially useful when dealing with difficult thoughts and feelings—the ones that make us feel *stuck* in the experience—the ones that we cannot separate ourselves from—the "storm" or "swirl" inside us. The simple act of noting and naming our inner state helps to calm spiraling thoughts and emotions.

How does this work?

Remember how we talked in Chapter 7 about sounds rising and falling on their own? Picture yourself back in the garden. You'd hear a constant stream of sounds: a bird singing, an animal scurrying, an insect buzzing, wind rustling through the trees. Silence would be rare, as sounds naturally rise and fall in nature. You couldn't stop them, nor would you need to; they come and go on their own.

Now, imagine *naming* or labeling the sounds you hear. Birds singing. Bees buzzing. Wind blowing.

As you name the sounds, your mind naturally becomes focused and calm. You might even notice the moments between them—eventually becoming aware of the *space in which* all the sounds rise and fall.

Again, in the same way that sound is continually happening in the garden, thoughts, feelings, and sensations are the natural "soundscape" within our mind and body. The idea is not to stop this from happening—not to make it go away—but rather to simply notice it. To name what we notice. Not to label it good or bad. Not to ignore or exaggerate it. Not to judge it or add a story to it. But rather to simply acknowledge and relax with what we are experiencing.

Once my friend Jessica began to notice her mean inner voice, she realized it showed up not just in her journal, but throughout the day. This unkind voice was berating her all the time.

As Jessica got better at identifying these critical thoughts, she named this voice "Bully." She decided that when she heard Bully, rather than engage in conversation with loathing, she would return to the discipline of Pausing.

She told me, "At first it was hard. It had been so automatic for so long; sometimes I didn't even recognize Bully as a different voice from mine. But I was determined to notice how Bully was separate from me. And I had to discipline myself to pay attention whenever that voice showed up. I had to discipline myself to Pause and Attend to myself as I noticed it."

She described how she would place her hand on her heart—Land, Arrive, Relax; the first LAR—and remind herself, *That is just Bully talking. And what Bully says is not the truth. You're okay, Jessica.*

This is how we Attend to ourselves.

Self-compassion is not *just* the act of noticing what is happening. It's the *additional* step of offering ourselves caring support. Like Ellen at the grocery store.

While it initially felt odd, it completely shifted the way Jessica met herself. Once she named this inner voice instead of engaging with it, her inner critic lost much of its power. Bully quieted, and so did her overall inner environment. This shift allowed Jessica to show up in the present in a whole new way.

Attending to ourselves during these inner "soundscapes" communicates that we are supported. Offering this type of kind attention is the way we practice self-compassion.

THE 90-SECOND RULE: UNDERSTANDING HOW EMOTIONS FLOW

Our emotions are more *fluid* than we think. Just like a sound in the forest, glittery snow flurries in the globe, or clouds moving through the sky, *emotions will rise and fall* in a rhythm of their own. What makes them seem so solid and fixed is our relationship to them, our "fixation" on them.

Brain scientist Dr. Jill Bolte Taylor, author of *My Stroke of Insight*, gave a wildly popular TED Talk where she explained that if we do not get into a "conversation" with our thoughts or emotions—if we don't try to avoid or exaggerate them, if we don't "add on" to them—they *will* rise and fall on their own. And we can see this illustrated through brain imaging, EEG, and blood chemistry.

Dr. Bolte Taylor shares, "When a person reacts to something in their environment, there's a 90-second chemical process that takes place in the body. After those 90 seconds, any lingering emotional response is the result of thoughts re-triggering the emotional circuit."

She explains that the moment we *perceive* a threat, it stimulates the corresponding emotional circuitry and triggers a physiological dump of stress hormones. She shares that unless the actual danger continues, either in real life or by engaging with a "story" about the danger, this hormone dump will flush through you in less than 90 seconds.

Ellen, the mom in the grocery store, seemed to understand that if she was able to ride out her feelings of frustration, or annoyance, or whatever her daughter's tantrums were triggering inside her, they would probably fall away by the time she got to the next aisle.

Bolte Taylor makes clear that the physiological reaction does not just apply when faced with external threats—real bears lurking in the woods, imagined pythons hiding in bushes, or children testing your patience—but it also occurs in reaction to our memories, as well as to our *feelings* about our memories.

She says, "There's probably a thought somewhere in your brain of somebody who did you wrong twenty years ago. Every time you think of that person it still starts that circuit."

But the circuit is fluid. Our emotions come and go. They don't stay the same for long. Not even for 91 seconds.

FEELING YOUR FEELINGS: EXPANDING YOUR EMOTIONAL CAPACITY

Many of us have never been taught that it is okay to *feel* the way we feel. Or to experience and honor our emotions as they arise. Our families, culture, and conditioning have taught us how to avoid, bury, or distrust our feelings.

We get all sorts of messages from other people to "not feel what we feel" as well as messages about which feelings are acceptable and which are not. *Look on the bright side. Be strong. How could you be mad at me?* These are all phrases that negate our feelings: Don't feel sadness; don't cry; don't be angry. Depending on your family, even "positive" or pleasant feelings may not be considered acceptable. *What are you so happy about* can send the message that it's not okay to feel joy.

We avoid feeling our emotions in so many ways. We absorb ourselves in mindless scrolling, consume ourselves in our to-do lists, and run around busy all the time until we exhaust ourselves. We binge on TV shows, drinking, eating, smoking, shopping—whatever we can do to *not feel.*

Rather than allowing ourselves to *feel* our emotions, we *think* about them. Or because of our resistance and fear of them, we simply experience anxiety. *A lot* of our anxiety is our *resistance* to *feeling* our feelings, which further distances us from any emotional experience in our bodies.

It's helpful to remember that emotions are just energy in motion, *e-motion*; and emotional energy starts in the body. When our heart races, or we feel queasy, or our palms sweat, or our heart aches—we are experiencing common physical indicators of emotion. Hiked shoulders, clenched jaw, tight fists—or even restlessness or fidgeting—can be the energy of an emotional experience. Physical sensations might be the energy of fear, anger, sadness, or a range of other emotions.

We are creating space to experience *feelings* rather than being overtaken by them. We are practicing naming it—noticing the experience we are having—acknowledging and allowing it.

We are training ourselves to notice our emotions and to progressively tolerate the *sensations* in our body so that we can be more present. To become curious enough to notice *what we are feeling as we are feeling it.*

We are learning to discover, sense, and compassionately acknowledge the tightness in our chest and constriction in our throat. Attending to ourselves as we explore:

- What is this sensation?
- How do I feel?
- What do I notice about my body right now?
- What is here?

As we do this gently and kindly, we are sending a message to ourselves that we can *be with* what is here. We can be present and supportive of ourselves and our experience—our pain and our joy.

So when we couple the Name Your Inner Experience with the Feel Your Feelings practice, it might look like this:

- Oh, my shoulders are hiked. Oh, my fists are tight. Oh, my jaw is clenched.
- Oh, thinking. Oh, anger. Oh, sadness.

We name and feel what is happening in our bodies while we simultaneously extend our care and warmth toward ourselves and our experience. We Attend to ourselves throughout the experience we are having—as we are having it.

Maybe we place our own hand on our heart as a gesture of compassion.

Maybe we remind ourselves, "*This* can be here, while I *also* Land, Arrive, Relax."

Maybe we say to ourselves, "I am okay. *All* of my feelings are welcome here."

Titrating Compassion

When we are having difficult feelings, it is almost impossible to trust that they will pass in 90 seconds. Or ever. But they will.

The care and warmth we offer ourselves are the essential ingredients that make this process possible. Our compassionate attitude creates the safety we need to fully experience our emotions as they arise.

Through incremental exposure to our sensations, if we are able to simultaneously stay grounded, breathe, and Relax on purpose, the nervous system will receive messages of *safety* that allow us to meet this experience in a new way.

Just as sensing support and feeling grounded are prerequisites for feeling safe, feeling cared for and connected creates another essential pathway to feelings of safety. Both are necessary steps in re-patterning our nervous system's response.

These practices expand our window of tolerance and help us learn to feel what we are experiencing in our bodies. When we feel safe enough to acknowledge our emotions, we can begin to understand what they may be telling us—and discover how best to express them. In these moments, we create the space to respond intentionally rather than react out of habit.

We are practicing Attending—offering gentle, kind, compassionate attention to ourselves and our emotions, cultivating the conditions we need to expand our behavioral options.

Creating Space to Feel Our Emotions

In her 1996 article "Growing Around Grief," Dr. Lois Tonkin used a great illustration to help us understand how we can learn to make space to *be with* our feelings, and even *feel* our feelings, while allowing ourselves to also experience, expand, and grow in our lives.

Dr. Tonkin shares the story of a mother who came to one of her workshops, whose child died years before. The woman described her journey of living with grief by drawing three illustrations.

The first illustration depicted a mason jar filled almost entirely by a single ball inside. The idea was to imagine the jar as yourself, with the ball symbolizing an overwhelming emotion, such as grief. In this first illustration, the grief ball completely fills the jar, vividly demonstrating the enormity of her grief, leaving little room for anything else. It represented how it first felt when she lost her child, how her grief dictated the way she felt, engaged with others, behaved on a daily basis, and experienced the world.

In the second illustration, she depicted how she thought she was supposed to, one day, get over her grief. She drew three mason jars, each jar the same size. But inside each jar was a grief ball of a different size. The first jar's ball was huge, fully encompassing the space. The second jar's ball got a little smaller. And the third jar's ball got smaller still. She thought her grief *should* progressively shrink and get smaller and smaller. Maybe, even one day, disappear. But this is *not* how it went at all.

She then illustrated her *actual* experience with a third drawing. In this picture, the balls did *not* shrink at all. Grief was still there, always the *same* size. But the jars were different. The first was the same as her earlier drawing, but the second and third jars were each progressively bigger. She showed how *she expanded*. She grew with and around her grief.

Little by little, as she became more capable of allowing herself to feel her grief, her fear of the sensations and emotions began to lessen. Staying present with her challenging emotions enabled her to widen her experience beyond grief into an expanded capacity to experience more of life.

These illustrations can help us understand how we can create space to be with and even feel our big, hard, challenging feelings. Rather than treating our emotions as something to get over—like a passing flu—they are an integral part of who we are. We are not trying to inoculate ourselves from our emotions. Or *graduate* from having them. Rather, we are actually expanding our capacity to experience and stay present with a wider range of human emotions.

Our emotions will come and go in their intensity. Our feelings will continue to rise and fall. They will get stirred up, swirl around, and, sometimes, even take over our container with their storm.

We can expect that we will feel engulfed by our emotions again. But we can practice remembering that we can always come back to the act of creating space to allow them to flow.

Emotions are called feelings because we experience them physically in the body. While emotions reside within the body, the thoughts we attach to them live in our mind.

Self-Compassion in Practice: Attending to Our Feelings

When we practice our first LAR (Land, Arrive, Relax), we are expanding our container so that we can tune in and be open to what we feel as we are feeling it.

As we practice our second LAR (Listen, Attend, Respond), we pay attention and Listen to what we find in our container. We are allowing what we feel to simply be what we feel. We Attend to ourselves and our experience. When we consciously add self-compassion, a gesture of our own loving support, we are letting ourselves know that our feelings are not something we need to "get over," but rather a human part of us that is welcome in our lives.

Susan, one of my students, was sixty-three years old when she told me that learning this LAR-LAR Pause practice helped her more than years of therapy. A few years earlier, Susan lost her life partner of thirty years in a tragic bike accident, and then her father suddenly passed away within a few months. She shared with me her experience of using LAR-LAR to support herself through her deep grief:

> I did not think I could physically live through my feelings. I thought I would surely have a heart attack from my heart pounding outside my chest or I would just lay on the floor and not be able to ever get up.
>
> I learned it was safe to experience my grief. I still think of the "Now, now Ellen" story. When I need to draw on it, I rub my chest in circles and say "Now, now, Susan." It helps calm me, slows down whatever fear or anxiety I am feeling, and makes me feel like I am no different than other people. I am not crazy, I am having a perfectly normal reaction to losing two people I loved so dearly.

Susan had been practicing LAR-LAR for six months when she wrote this. She also shared that she had not been in debilitating despair since learning to meet herself in this way, which she described as "remarkable."

When we Attend to ourselves, acknowledging whatever resides in our emotional container, we create space to notice, accept, and feel what is present with loving awareness. In doing so, we foster a sense of feeling seen, received, and loved.

This leaves us feeling more safe.

The Science of Compassion

Kristin Neff, author of *Self-Compassion: The Proven Power of Being Kind to Yourself*, has shown that offering ourselves compassion helps us feel not only more safe in our nervous system, but also less defensive overall, supporting us in being more open and flexible in our response to our circumstances and the environment.

Scientists describe how self-compassion is an active ingredient that allows us to shift the nervous system and change our neurology. Compassion can help soothe the amygdala and limbic system—our fear circuitry—while turning on the prefrontal cortex, the part of our brain needed to expand into big-picture awareness and thinking, ultimately enabling us to choose our response in the moment.

Self-compassion also positively impacts our physiology in equal measure. Our heart rate and breathing rate lower, our muscle tone softens, and our hormones shift to the ones that support our ability to *feel* more connected. Our cortisol levels decrease, and oxytocin is released. Oxytocin, sometimes described as a "bonding" hormone because it increases positive feelings of love and connection, helps us feel more compassion.

Oxytocin is released in large amounts during birth and breastfeeding. It helps regulate mother-baby bonding, but it turns out it's not just mothers. A less well-known fact is that fathers, when interacting with their infants, also experience a rise in oxytocin equal to that of mothers.

We are designed to receive boosts of bonding-related hormones each time we feel cared for and loved.

Research also shows that practicing compassion for *ourselves* boosts levels of oxytocin, dopamine, and serotonin, not only sending our nervous system messages of safety, but also lifting our mood and further enhancing a sense of connectedness and belonging.

And amazingly, compassion—whether it comes from someone else or *ourselves*—leaves us feeling Listened to and Attended to. When we feel Listened to, the part of the brain that lights up is the same part that lights up when we feel loved. And when we *don't* feel Listened to, the opposite is true.

What's more, science shows that when we Attend to ourselves compassionately, it shifts our neurological and physiological response exponentially in our favor to *do it again*. To repeat it. Meaning, the next time we experience our own vulnerability, Attending to ourselves will be more accessible. Compassion begets compassion. And it ups the odds that we will be able to send a message of loving support to ourselves in the future.

So, how we meet ourselves in the moment, changes our behavior.

Which changes the future . . .

We can use our emotions for guidance about connection, relationships, and extending more tender care to ourselves and others. They can also guide us when we need to be more clear with actions to create boundaries, meet challenges, and even leave a situation.

Listening and Attending: Expanding Our Response

Let's take a moment to review. Listening is a skill in itself, but to truly listen, we must also cultivate the ability to create space for what we hear. Ultimately, that is the practice of Attending.

We actively practice Landing, Arriving, and Relaxing *as we Listen*—so that we are better able to regulate our nervous system. As we *simultaneously* Attend to ourselves throughout our experience, we are supporting ourselves neurologically to stay open with what we *hear and feel*—rather than getting hijacked by the habit of reacting to our emotional experience.

We need to feel safe and grounded in order to be present enough to notice what is happening inside and around us. We need to *allow* what arises and not add on. And we need to do all this in such a gentle, kind, friendly way that our body and mind feel like it's all okay. That we feel safe, supported, and loved. We do this through Attending.

We now know that thoughts and feelings will rise and fall on their own over 90 seconds if we can turn our attention toward the physical sensations in our body rather than the "stories" that fuel our painful emotions. Every time we Pause to Listen and Attend to ourselves, we can create conditions to expand our ability to be more present and open to our full range of human experiences. All the "feels" . . . even the hard ones.

We are learning to set conditions to return, over and over again, to meet ourselves compassionately, all day long. Every day. We know it's only a matter of time before the next challenge arrives—whether it's a difficult phone call, unsettling email, financial setback, or disagreement. External stresses will always continue to flow our way.

We are practicing re-wiring the way we meet ourselves. We are practicing meeting ourselves softly, kindly, and curiously. Over and over, one breath at a time, we ask ourselves, "How can I care for myself right now?" "What do I need right now?" "How can I Attend to myself, right here and right now, so I can skillfully and wisely choose my response?"

Emotions as Guides

As we learn to *allow* ourselves to *feel* what we feel, with whatever is present, we are able to grow more conscious of *how* we feel. And as we get more familiar with *feeling how* we feel, we can also grow more aware of what our emotions are trying to tell us. We can better discern when our emotions are giving us important insight and information about our needs and safety—as emotions can ultimately offer us feedback to help us to tap into whatever wisdom we may need to know in the moment.

As we create space to know what we are feeling, rather than ignore it or exaggerate it, we can validate it. Then we can receive more of what this emotion is here to tell us. And as we grow more conscious about how our emotions make us feel, we may also become more aware of our habitual reactions *to* them. It becomes easier to notice when we are escalating unnecessarily or how we instantly armor up to protect ourselves. We can get to know when and how we close down, or what we need in order to open up.

As we become more familiar with our emotions and our inner experience, we can become more clear and honest about what we are carrying into each moment—and into our relationships—that may not be about the present conditions. We have more of what we need to choose our response.

PAUSE TO PRACTICE ATTENDING

For the purposes of putting this in book form, I have separated the skills of Listening and Attending, but in practice, we do them in tandem. We discover what is happening and attend to ourselves *as we are experiencing it*. For it is the way we meet what we discover that creates the conditions for change. Remember, it is the *way that we meet ourselves* that will leave us feeling more safe to soften and open—or leave us feeling as though we have to protect ourselves further, causing us to harden or close down.

- To begin, notice where your body meets support. Consider that besides whatever is under you, there is also the whole planet, our Earth, holding you up. Our Earth is always holding you, just as you are. On your next exhale, let yourself Land in your body on the Earth, in the spot where you are.
- Allow your breath to Arrive in your body. *Feel* your breath Arrive in your body. Mentally trace the path of your breath as it flows through you. Allow your mind, allow *yourself*, to Arrive on the flow of the breath. Arriving with *this* inhale; Arriving with *this* exhale. The breath is always present, flowing through you, just as you are. Here. Now.
- As you allow the ground to hold you and the breath to flow through you, Relax on purpose. On your next exhale, you might allow your jaw to dangle, your shoulders to fall away from your ears, fists to unfurl. Relax any areas you may be unnecessarily gripping or guarding. Release the extra work, excess effort, inner squeezing, that is not needed right now.

Soften anything you can. On each breath, continually allow yourself to Relax a little bit more.

- For the next few breaths, gently expand your awareness, your Listening, to notice what is happening inside of you. Simply notice any thoughts, feelings, sensations you may be having.
- Practice not adding judgment or harshness or anything else on top of what you discover. Perhaps you might just name what you discover for what it is. Not to label good or bad, just to simply acknowledge it. Something like: Oh, my shoulders are hiked. Oh, my fists are tight. Oh, my heart feels heavy. Oh, thinking. Oh, anger. Oh, sadness. Oh, numbness.

As you Listen, simply acknowledge what is present, and Attend to yourself and what you find.

- Attend to yourself and your experience, as you discover whatever is happening here, now. Whatever you may encounter—thoughts, feelings, sensations—simply notice it and let it be known—felt—for what it is. You don't need to make anything different, or make it go away, or stop it. Whatever we encounter, we simply notice it and *let it be known, felt, for what it is*. Then, we hold what we find in our open, caring awareness.

Maybe we place our own hand on our heart as a gesture of compassion.

Maybe we remind ourselves, "*This* can be here, while I *also* Land, Arrive, Relax."

Maybe we say to ourselves, "I am okay. *All* of my feelings are welcome here. I am welcome here, *just as I am*."

- Remember we are not trying to "change" anything. Rather, as we find what we find, we can Attend to ourselves throughout the experience we are having—as we are having it. Meeting ourselves with kindness. We are creating a kind, compassionate space for ourselves. Just as we are.
- To close, return to feel your body held up by support, the earth. Feel your breath moving in your body. Re-relax. Set an intention to check back in with yourself throughout the day. To caringly come back to Listen and Attend to yourself, again and again.

WHEN YOU NEED MORE SUPPORT WITH LISTENING AND ATTENDING

If you need more prompting, you might ask yourself: How am I today? Right now? What inside me needs attention, acceptance, support? How can I care for myself right now?

May you be gentle and kind
with yourself.
May you forgive yourself.
May you Attend to your own heart.
Just as you are now.

CHAPTER 9

Respond

When I teach a retreat on learning to Pause and we start talking about Responding, it's the part of the workshop where I offer the least amount of "curriculum." Because the skills we've learned to date—LAR-LA—are the skills we need to be grounded, open, present, and ready to choose how we wish to Respond *in the moment.*

What each moment brings—what unfolds in real time—is inherently unique to each of us.

I can teach someone how to feel their feet on the ground, take a mindful breath, and loosen the tension in their shoulders. I can teach people how to listen deeply and meet themselves with compassion. But I cannot tell anyone what their most wise and considered Response should be.

Instead, I offer the guidance to *experience* the Pause. The space in which we can become more intentional in the way we Respond to the moment—even as we are simultaneously aware of the habitual reactions that might be pulling us.

It is in this space that we have time and perspective to not only notice how we *feel*, but to also grow aware of what we always have done and what we might now do differently. And it is also in this space that we can take the time we need to choose our Response.

Back at the Table

As I shared in Chapter 2, I was in the middle of raging in my bathroom when I suddenly realized that *I had left the table*—and it dawned on me that the only one who was going to be able to change *my* situation was *me*.

After taking my Landing, Arriving, and Relaxing breaths a few times, I calmed down and was able to go back down into the kitchen, back to the table with a more open heart and a desire to reconnect.

My mind had settled, and my breath was steady. My mother and daughter were still at the table chatting. My mother had a look on her face that to me read *let's just move forward like nothing happened*. Willow seemed rigid and ready to get right back into it. I could understand why she might expect a fight.

I noticed how uncomfortable I felt and put my hand on my heart. I couldn't name the tangle of emotions inside me, only that they were far from pleasant. I acknowledged to myself, *I am struggling right now*, and I took another breath and softened.

Pausing, I Listened. Pausing, I Attended to myself.

Listen. Attend.

Listen. Attend.

Meeting myself in this way calmed me more than even I expected it to.

I looked into Willow's eyes and apologized for snapping. Her face softened, although she still looked a little skeptical.

I asked her if I could share my experience. Willow agreed to hear me out.

"Your comment to Grandma sounded insulting and hurtful. To me, it felt mean," I said.

We all sat in silence for an eternal moment before she responded.

Willow said, "I can see how maybe my comment could have sounded mean. Maybe I said that to Grandma because of what you said to me. I was so mad at *you*."

Dumbfounded, I could feel myself getting hot again. *What I said to her?* What did *I* do wrong?

I looked over at my mother and it seemed like she was holding her breath for what was about to happen next.

On the spot, I regrounded with the first LAR, Pausing to calm myself all over again.

"Please tell me, what did I say?" I asked Willow with genuine curiosity. With my stress response quelled, I was more primed to truly want to Listen and understand her experience.

Reflectively, she said, "You said something earlier in our conversation that really hurt." She continued to share what I said . . . and sure enough, I could see how *my* comment had been hurtful. "I guess I got angry from that point on," she finished.

As I write this, I have tried to remember the exact conversation, the exact words that were exchanged, but the fact is, what I said at the table hurt my daughter, and that's really the only thing that is important. We all say things to the people we love that are sometimes insensitive or thoughtless. We all hear things as slights sometimes, whether they were intended that way or not.

We are always moving into our next moment based on our experience of the previous moment. Our next moment is shaped by how we participate in the one before it.

When we are habitually stuck in the stress response, it is normal to listen defensively—to assume that someone is trying to be hurtful. And this is not because we are oversensitive. It is because it is *hard* to Pause and give something real consideration in a moment when we instantly feel like we are under attack.

My daughter had been upset by my words, but my genuine curiosity toward her in this moment allowed her to reflect rather than defend.

She finished with, "Honestly, I might have said what I did to Grandma, to hurt you. I guess I did mean to be mean—not to Grandma, but to *you*."

Ugh. I felt terrible (and ashamed) about my own mindless and hurtful behavior. Again, I Paused and took a deep breath as I felt my hand on my heart. I apologized once more.

Willow's face softened more as she acknowledged my sincerity. She also apologized to me, and to my mother.

My mom finally began to breathe. It was clear that she, too, was relieved. "Wow, that was truly something," she said with a big exhale.

Reaction Versus Response

As I reflect on the night at the table, I could see how my own jump to defensiveness was so organic. Willow's offensive comment to my mother triggered my fight-or-flight response and a feeling that I needed to protect my mom. This instinct felt familiar, even historic, as I had often viewed my mother as a victim of my father, a perception that shaped many of my early experiences, as I've mentioned.

This old pattern fueled anger in the moment and an impulse to control Willow's behavior. But rather than escalate or engage in the conflict, I escaped the situation and stormed upstairs, instinctively retreating to someplace safe—something I often did as a child when the stress kicked up in my home.

This is not only a normal, adaptive reaction when someone feels threatened, but it's also often a good choice. Reacting is an immediate, instinctive, impulsive action influenced by our nervous system—especially our past experiences or fears. Driven by emotions, reactions are part of our most primitive survival system and quickly become habitual to help us act without "thinking." When we're under stress or feeling threatened, the amygdala can take over our brain, leading to impulsive reactions instead of conscious responses—circumstances where understanding—or reparation—cannot take place (at least not at that moment).

Response-Ability

While automatic physiological reactions may help save us during life-threatening danger, when navigating day-to-day difficulties or struggling with non-life-threatening challenges in relationships, it's more helpful to have the ability to Respond. Our response-ability.

In contrast to our impulsive immediate reactions, Responding is a thoughtful and deliberate action. It involves mindfulness—awareness of the situation, consideration of the options, and conscious decision making.

Responses are our *intentional choices.*

But we are so used to living life as a series of reactions to whatever is going on around us that we often don't even know we have a *choice.*

Frequently overwhelmed by life and by our circumstances, we are stuck on a hamster wheel, getting through, day by day, the same way. We become stuck in the same habits, reactions, and, therefore, situations—for years, decades, or even a lifetime. We repeat our thinking patterns—in loops of self-criticism, feelings of unworthiness, and fortified stories of blame, resentment, and disappointment—reinforcing our *feelings of being stuck* in so many aspects of our lives.

Most of the time, we are trying to figure out how to get unstuck. We look for ways out of our stress, discomfort, anxiety, and pain by trying to figure out how to make the world different, others different, and our circumstances different. This is a stance of reaction—a natural impulse based on our fear circuitry. However, there's another way to make things different, based not on our stress, but on our clarity. And that is our ability to Respond to things exactly as they are.

Practicing our first LAR enables us to regulate our fear circuitry and creates the conditions we need to move into the second LAR—where we can recognize and experience our feelings without being hijacked by our habitual reactions. Through practice, we may grow our capacity to recognize our feelings and even come to know their triggers, while also choosing to support ourselves throughout the process—all essential components of a conscious Response.

As we Listen and Attend to ourselves, we are sending a message *to ourselves* that we are safe, allowing our minds to shift into a new conversation: *What is really happening here? What are my options right now? How do I wish to Respond?*

After using LAR-LAR in my bathroom, I could go back to the table and engage with my daughter in a way that I would not have been capable of just a few minutes earlier. And more importantly, I *wanted* to engage with her.

So, while fleeing is part of our survival instinct, it can also be a wise choice, granting us time and space to eventually calm down and re-regulate. Taking a pause—physically stepping away or mentally detaching for a moment—creates the space we need to reset. This brief interruption allows us to return with renewed calm, clarity, and openness, which are necessary ingredients for fostering change, repairing relationships, and promoting growth.

IMAGINED REACTIONS CAN HELP RELEASE STUCK E-MOTIONS: AN EXERCISE

There may be times when we try to Pause but can't because we feel too overwhelmed with strong feelings. Or maybe we try to Pause but find we are numb and unsure of what we are actually feeling. These kinds of habitual emotional patterns prevent us from being able to choose our Response. Instead, we may benefit from dissipating some of the energy that is pent up in our bodies before we begin to consider our Response.

When you aren't able to properly express your emotions or move them through your body—if you don't feel safe, or if the context or environment isn't appropriate, or if you're in the habit of resisting or repressing emotions—you might try *imagining* how you would release those emotions. Similar to conscious relaxation, we can use visualization to change the state of our mind and body and start the process of putting that energy into motion.

To do this, begin with the first LAR to set a foundation of stability. Then *Listen* to how you feel and allow yourself to imagine how you might express those feelings if you could. There's no wrong way, so even if something feels new or silly you can try it out in the privacy of your own mind. For instance, if you are feeling angry, you might imagine yelling—you don't even have to yell *words*, just making a sound counts! If you are feeling sad, you might imagine crying or perhaps receiving a supportive hug from a caring friend.

Do this without overexaggerating the reaction; simply visualize expressing it *just enough* to allow the energy of the emotion to move through you. Do this for just a few minutes, or until you feel complete, then take several breaths to Attend to yourself and the emotions you have just processed. Finish with a full LAR-LAR practice.

This visualization exercise can help to reduce the intensity of your emotions, or help you identify how you are feeling, while setting conditions to create a little more clarity and space to eventually Respond more mindfully. In Chapter 15, I offer several somatic movement practices that can complement this exercise and further help us in these situations—especially if you are working with high anxiety or trauma.

It's Okay Not to Know

Many of us imagine that in order to Respond on purpose, we need to "know" how to respond in advance. Or we believe that we should only Respond when we know the "right" response. However, responding doesn't require knowing all the answers to whatever may arise. In fact, it's often better to *not know* in advance.

When I teach this in retreats, I ask my students to use some imagery about circumstances they have been in before or know they are likely to be in soon. As we visualize these scenarios, we *practice* Responding.

And, even though we make a plan, how we Respond in the moment may be different than what we had imagined we might do. LAR-LA sets us up to be ready to Respond more mindfully to whatever the moment may call for.

When it comes to Responding, the only thing I know for sure is that there is no "should."

We don't need to figure everything out. We just need to give ourselves space to hear and Listen to others—and the world around us—while we also receive our own thoughts or feelings.

Even when things are uncomfortable, if we can trust the ground to support us, we can open more fully to what we discover. We simply need to allow ourselves to Listen.

As we expand our awareness into the present, we are simultaneously practicing curiosity and nonjudgmental attention. Learning to be with things *the way they are*, rather than the way we want them to be, gives us the space to choose our Response not only from our mind, but also from our heart.

I know that the idea of responding from our heart can seem like a fluffy, new-age concept, but it's an ancient concept and one worth understanding.

In many East Asian languages, the word for "mind" and the word for "heart" are the *same*. The Chinese word *xin* refers to the physical heart as well as to the mind, which makes sense, because the ancient Chinese regarded the heart as being at the center of human cognition.

Pausing allows us access to this *heart-mind* relationship. Once we feel grounded, we are able to Listen more deeply, moment by moment, and be with things as they are.

In this sense, we are truly befriending ourselves and our experience. As we bring ourselves into the present this way, we set the neurological conditions needed to Listen more openly to what we hear.

Again and Again . . .

But still, the big question is, how do we *repeatedly* welcome *whatever* is going on inside us and around us? Even the big, big stuff? This question arises because, unfortunately, it's not as if we can regulate ourselves once or twice and be done with it. We must cultivate the habit of *continually* Landing (getting grounded), Arriving (breathing into what we notice), Relaxing our body in the places we habitually armor up, and making space for whatever shows up without judging it or ourselves. And we do all of this knowing that in the next hour, the next day—the next minute—we may invariably find ourselves stressed again.

Reacting again.

The idea is that we are setting the conditions to make our choice in real time based both on what we are experiencing as well as opening to what is *actually* happening in the present moment. And in this moment. And this moment. And this one.

Moment-to-Moment Updates

I love the Global Positioning System (GPS) app, Waze. It gives you continually updated directions for the best route to your destination. But I often drive with a friend who doesn't like using Waze, or trust in GPSes overall. This friend always insists they know exactly where they're going and the best way to get there. The *right* way.

But rarely is there only one way.

The cool thing about Waze, and many of today's GPSes, is that it also takes into account a variety of perspectives and experiences. The directions suggested by the GPS are not solely based on an "aerial view" of the route and surrounding area (which we simply cannot see from our vantage point in our car), but they *also* take into consideration the input and experience of other drivers on the very same route.

In addition, the directions are continuously updating the most current conditions, which change by the moment. A good reminder that even if we know the best way to go at any given time, conditions along that route can change at any given time.

Everything can change at any given time.

Yet, change is rarely welcomed by the nervous system, which seeks comfort in predictability and familiarity. Despite this natural resistance, change remains an inevitable and essential part of reality.

Because change *will* continually occur, all day long, it's wise to remember to Pause—*all day long.* Pausing will help us reorient and re-regulate several times a day so we can be present and open to the conditions that have just "updated." So that we can calmly ask ourselves: *How are things* now? *What am I experiencing* now? *What do I need to know* now?

Pausing for Guidance and Insight

We don't save Pausing for the high stakes moments in our lives, or challenging conversations, or when we are at a crossroads. All day long we are making decisions and choices and taking actions. And all day long we have access to guidance bigger than our habitual thinking can offer.

My dear teacher and friend Erich Schiffmann, renowned yoga master and author of *Yoga: The Spirit and Practice of Moving into Stillness*, once told a story at a teacher training program to help us understand how Pausing and Listening for guidance in the small moments of our life is the very training we need to access wisdom on a regular basis.

Erich shared that he was at the grocery store with his regular weekly shopping list but decided to tuck the list away in his pocket and practice Pausing and choosing what he might want to buy today, rather than filling his cart with all the usual things. Erich was in the fruit aisle, about to pick up his favorite Macintosh apples, but instead, he Paused and looked at the wide array of apples available. For a moment, he got grounded, took a breath, and wondered: *Today, should I buy the red Macintoshes? Or should I buy the Fuji, or the Gala, or the Honeycrisp?*

Erich described himself as a red-apple lover, yet he unexpectedly perked up when he got to the green Granny Smiths. He never bought green apples, but his urge was so strong he put the Granny Smiths in the cart and wheeled on.

Erich did this again in the bread aisle, surprised by the pull to buy white bread over his usual twelve-grain loaf. But he went with it.

Later that afternoon, his grandmother came with a friend for an unannounced visit. And it just so turned out that not only was Grandma's friend allergic to all red apples and could only eat green ones, but his grandmother also preferred white bread for her sandwich, which he normally would not have on hand.

We are often so habitual about our choices and behavior, even in things like what we eat for lunch, that we don't pause and consider opening space for other options. And beyond what we might eat for lunch, we can practice being less habitual and opening space for guidance and intuition in all areas of our life. Erich often says, "Don't make your decisions alone. Pause, open your mind, ask for guidance, notice what you are prompted to do."

You might not hear a "voice" telling you what to do, but you just might be pulled to do something differently than you normally do, or than you think you should do, or than you want to do. You may not even know for sure why you are pulled to do something at the time.

I'll never forget Robin, who was a student on one of my earliest retreats. We were in the midst of a Pausing meditation when Robin experienced a very strong impulse to call her mother.

Robin immediately left class and called her mom right at that moment. She and her mom shared a few minutes of sweet conversation. Robin felt reassured and was about to get off the call when her mother suddenly went silent. Robin heard the sound of her mother falling, hung up, and immediately called emergency services. She later learned that her mother had had a stroke. Had Robin not been on the phone with her at that very time, she wouldn't have been able to call emergency services for help for her mother, who lived alone on a farm, ultimately saving her life.

We won't always know in advance why we get strong impulses to act. The more we practice Pausing and Listening—whether it is buying a different apple or calling a loved one or anything in between—the more we open ourselves to a sense of "knowing" beyond our "thinking mind" alone.

When we slow down, get grounded, present, and open, we are better able to receive new insights and guidance, so that we can become more responsive to whatever comes our way.

Maybe It's Not the Whole Story

As we bring more awareness and openness to our present-moment conditions, we may find that we may also be able to be more neutral, or to have more of the clear, nonjudgmental equanimity of Attending. Equanimity is also part of Responding and helps us create more ease and readiness in our body and our mind. Like curiosity, it helps us to stay present, and more pliable, while we allow things to unfold further.

Like compassion, equanimity is a choice, not a predetermined state. When we are so attached to wanting things to be a certain way, especially wanting them different from what they are, we can't possibly make a wise decision because we just don't know the whole story yet. Equanimity broadens our perspective to receive more information and insight and decide how to act.

There is a Chinese proverb about a farmer and his son. The son had a beloved stallion who helped the family earn a living.

One day, the horse ran away and their neighbors exclaimed, "Your horse ran away, what terrible luck!"

The farmer replied, "Maybe so, maybe not. We'll see."

A few days later, the horse returned home, leading a few wild mares back to the farm along with him. The neighbors shouted, "Your horse has returned, and brought several horses home with him. What great luck!"

The farmer replied, "Maybe so, maybe not. We'll see."

Later that week, the farmer's son was trying to break one of the mares and she threw him to the ground, fracturing the boy's leg. The villagers cried, "Your son broke his leg, what terrible luck!"

The farmer replied, “Maybe so, maybe not. We’ll see.”

A few weeks later, soldiers from the national army came to recruit all able-bodied boys for the army. They did not take the farmer’s son, who was still recovering from his fall. Friends shouted, “Your boy is spared; what tremendous luck!”

The farmer replied, “Maybe so, maybe not. We’ll see.”

The farmer is Responding with equanimity here.

Rather than thinking we know how things are, or limiting our minds with our assumptions, assessments, judgments, and reactions . . . rather than adding more confusion with our stories, opinions, or consuming ourselves in worry, anticipation, anxiety, we can Pause and allow the moment to be just what it is. We can do this even in a challenging moment, in the heat of the moment, when we don’t like the way things are.

More often than not, we really don’t know why things are happening the way they are. Allowing ourselves to Pause can calm us and enable us to open our minds for more possibility. We untangle ourselves. We back up, over and over again, to re-ground and re-open. We expand our capacity to let things unfold a little bit, to see more clearly, and to open to insight and wisdom so that we can Respond in the moment freshly—differently.

Responding All Day Long

All day long we are confronted by moments we need to Respond to, whether it is choosing what goes into our grocery cart or how we respond when we are anxious, angry, or hurt. Or when someone else is anxious, angry, or hurt. Or in a difficult conversation with the people closest to us at the table.

I don't know what *your* choice will be. And, if you're doing the practice, you most likely won't know in advance what your choice will be either.

You may choose to LAR-LA all over again—before you are ready to Respond.

You may choose to "not Respond," but rather be quiet, and listen more.

You may choose to create boundaries. Or leave a situation altogether.

You may choose to speak up. Advocate for yourself or another.

Express your disappointment and hurt.

Apologize.

You may choose to make the phone call. To end a phone call.

You may choose to leave a job. Take a job.

Leave a relationship. Start a relationship.

Have the piece of cake. Not have the cake.

Buy the apples. Not buy the apples.

Pausing allows us to be curious about what is happening in the moment—inside us and around us. Then, moment by moment, we can choose how we wish to Respond.

Practicing More Caring Responses

When I was sequestered in the bathroom and finally Paused, I recognized the familiar weight of old pain surfacing. Under the defensive stance of my hiked-up shoulders were historic feelings of fear and sadness from growing up in a household filled with violent shouting and aggression. Fear that my mother was under attack. Fear that I was not safe. This was still alive in me—even while I felt the pain of the immediate situation.

In order to truly make a new choice, we need to feel what is happening inside us. To connect with the present more openly, we first learn to connect with ourselves. We need to discover what we feel. Not what we *think* we feel. What we actually feel.

Name our experience. Feel our experience. Attend to ourselves with whatever we find. This sets the conditions to Respond.

It's easy to see how my reaction to what Willow said could have gone differently. Maybe you can relate, but for me, it initially feels more powerful to hold on to my *story* about how I am right and someone else is wrong.

Despite our discomfort, our brains are better at noticing and amplifying our hurt, pain, or anger. Our sadness, disconnection, or disappointments. And this is okay. We are not trying to *get rid of* our feelings or the current conditions we find ourselves in. We Pause and Attend to ourselves *with* the present conditions, not despite them.

We can disrupt the usual patterns that keep us stuck—whether it's holding on to our "rightness," clinging to unworthiness, or unconsciously protecting ourselves through negative self-talk. Had I not returned to the table, the difficult conversation with my family would have caused more wounds, continuing the cycle.

Small moments like these accumulate, leaving us repeatedly feeling stressed and threatened. These unconscious reactions trap us in old narratives and limiting beliefs, blocking our capacity for growth and evolution.

It is easy to see how quickly our pain and stress habits get passed along, even unintentionally.

We do this all day long. With those we love and with those we don't even know. And especially with those we don't favor. It may be hard to imagine, but our dysregulation has consequences for everyone we come into contact with.

We don't Pause to feel *relaxed* (though it may often feel good to do so); we Pause to have a more responsive and flexible nervous system.

Practicing mindful, compassionate Responses benefits both us and those around us.

Response in Action

My student Jenn gave me permission to share something she wrote, perfectly illustrating the power of practicing LAR-LAR:

> Walking into my first workshop with Jillian at Kripalu Center for Yoga and Health in Massachusetts, my hands shook with anxiety. I was halfway across the country from my home in Wisconsin, and I felt like the dry, empty hull of a seed.
>
> My young sons were two and five years old. The aching beauty of new motherhood, yet also the repetitive, monotonous daily routine, was at odds with my previous life of variety as a freelance writer. I felt like I was running at a constant sprint, which had turned into a never-ending race that I could never win.
>
> During the week of teachings and practice, I soaked in Jillian's gentle instructions and the science supporting them. We practiced learning to Pause with LAR-LAR, over and over—on mindful walks in the woods, on our yoga mats, standing in line for dinner. I was sometimes able to remember to pause; when I did, my body felt stable and safe, and my mind and heart were able to communicate more clearly.

Sometimes new paths of thought and action—or a choice not to act—appeared that I hadn't been able to see before.

Leaving the workshop, I felt transformed. I have always been an anxious traveler, fussing about being late or any of a million other things out of my control. But on this trip, I felt stable, peaceful, able to stop and practice LAR-LAR when I needed to. On my flight home, this would make a world of difference to me and to a total stranger.

The first leg of my trip from the East Coast to Detroit was fine. However, our second flight to Minneapolis was delayed and delayed, until it was finally canceled at 11:00 p.m. Ordinarily, I would have been at anxiety level eleven, tired from a long day of travel, heartsick at not being able to get home that night, missing my husband and boys, all alone to sort this out for myself.

But because I had been practicing LAR-LAR, I was able to access the pause. And it felt magical—miraculous even. As the line formed at the ticket desk, as people around me grumbled and cursed, I didn't spin out. I didn't feel flooded and overwhelmed. I was stunned. It was not only that my mind was calm—there was no physical adrenaline or cortisol spike in my chest, no tightness in my stomach, no racing heartbeat.

I stepped out of the line of passengers waiting for hotel and meal vouchers, allowing everyone else to go ahead of me. I sent mental hugs to the families with little kids my sons' age who were struggling with exhaustion and frustration. I said an internal "thank you" to the gate agent, who was being so patient with the upset crowd. I waited until every other passenger, except for one woman, had gone through the line. When I finally approached the desk, I overheard the woman desperately talking on her cell phone and trying to talk to the gate agent at the same time. Neither conversation was going well. I noticed that she spoke Spanish on her phone call. I felt my feet on the ground. I took a breath. I relaxed on purpose.

My first husband was Colombian, and I still speak Spanish fluently. I touched the woman on the shoulder and asked: "*Disculpe, Señora, pero habla usted Español?*" ("Excuse me, ma'am, but do you speak Spanish?") She turned around, and her face registered relief and happiness as she heard familiar words.

She didn't speak very much English and hadn't understood what was happening with the flight. Her name was Justa, and she was a Peruvian grandmother (*abuela*) traveling from New York to Minnesota for her grandson's birthday.

I was so grounded that I didn't race to action—I just went step by step. She handed me her cell phone so I could talk to her daughter in Minnesota. I explained that we were supposed to get a voucher and take a shuttle to a hotel, then shuttle back for a new flight in the morning. The three of us decided that Abuela Justa and I would navigate the rest of the night—and the trip—together. Just past midnight, the gate agent gave us vouchers to stay at an airport hotel and off we went to find the shuttles. I walked her to her room, and we said goodnight for the few hours of sleep we had ahead.

We woke before dawn and went back to the airport, boarding our flight while talking about Peruvian food, summers in Minnesota, and winters in New York. The flight was fine, and we walked to baggage claim together. I truly felt like we were family.

I gathered all our bags—hers containing precious Peruvian foods for the party—and we walked out to arrivals to meet her family. Her husband and her grandson ran to give her hugs, then wrapped me up in huge, grateful hugs as well. Justa made the sign of the cross over my forehead and heart many times, saying, "*Que dios te bendiga, y que dios les bendiga siempre a sus hijos y su familia.*" ("May God bless you, and may God always bless your children and your family.") We asked someone to take a quick picture of us all together. Then Justa whispered in Spanish: "You are an angel from God who came to help me. Thank you, God." They got into their car and left, Justa and her grandson waving until they were out of sight.

This incredible experience never could have happened without the transformation of learning to Pause. LAR-LAR allowed me to stay with myself, be open to other people, and to access my own light, perception, and best self. Pausing empowered me to be of service to someone else. Instead of fear and anxiety, there was peace and safety for her, for me, and for her family, in both New York and Minnesota.

Abuelita Justa and I still text each other a few times a year to say hello. The memory of that trip makes me feel so grateful. I am thankful for the unexpected beauty and paths in life, and so thankful for the powerful possibilities contained in practicing LAR-LAR.

THE 90-SECOND, SIX-BREATH LAR-LAR PRACTICE

The first three breaths, the first LAR, is *how* you Pause. The second three breaths, the second LAR, is how you can expand your awareness in the space of the Pause. Where we can meet ourselves and the conditions we are in with presence and compassion; create clarity and open ourselves to insight; and create conditions to choose how we will participate, or Respond, in the moment.

- To begin, sense the support underneath your body. On your next breath, feel where your body *meets* the support. Exhaling, let your body Land on the earth, in the spot where you are. Land.
- Feel your next breath Arrive in your body. As you exhale, let your mind rest on the flow of the breath. Arriving here. Now.
- On your next breath, allow yourself to Relax any unnecessary gripping, holding, or clenching you notice. Exhaling, soften your jaw, shoulders, hands.
- On your next breath, Listen. Simply notice any thoughts, feelings, or sensations you may be having—without adding anything else on top of what you discover. Exhaling, allow yourself to simply be present with what you notice.
- On your next breath, Attend to yourself and your experience, as you discover whatever is happening here, now. Kindly, *let it be known—felt—for what it is*. You may want to place a hand on your heart as a gesture of compassion. Or offer yourself a word of support.

- On your next breath, acknowledge any clarity for your Response, which may have already risen inside you now.

You may experience a deep prompt or pull guiding you to Respond. Or you may need to ask your *Self*—your deep inner knowing—for a little more guidance. If you need more prompting, ask yourself:

- How might I best Respond here, now?
- What does my Body say?
- What does my Heart say?
- What does my Mind say?
- What does my Higher Self say?
- What does my Soul say?

To close, stay present with yourself as you move into the next moment. Set an intention to be present with your inner experience even as you engage with others or the world around you. And an intention to Pause again for a full LAR-LAR practice a few times during your day.

Practicing All Day, Every Day: What Do I Need to Know Right Now?

Pausing for guidance on Responding throughout your day is key to gaining confidence in your ability to Respond. It helps us to build our Response muscle and trust in the process. It's easy to fall back on "shoulds" and "habits," so checking in more regularly, all day long, with open-ended questions can develop our Response-ability skills and access them more easily in the heat of the moment.

Each morning, begin your day with the LAR-LAR practice. I also vote for Pausing several times a day. Perhaps before each meal. Or even set your phone alarm for every four hours or so. Each time you reach the Respond step, ask your Self (or the general universe) the open-ended question, *What do I need to know right now?* (Thank you Erich Schiffmann for teaching me this). This question is not for the purpose of getting an immediate answer. Instead, the purpose and power of this question is in the asking. It's a curious and gentle question that opens us up to the wisdom inside us, and makes us better able to receive the wisdom that may come our way from those around us. When we Listen in this way, it shifts how we Listen in the world. It serves to align our head with our heart, and supports us in choosing our most wise and compassionate Response—from one moment to the next.

May we remember
our Response ripples out—
and can affect everyone we come
into contact with.
May we remember that Pausing
is an act of Love.

PART TWO

LIVING

In this section, we will learn how pausing can impact and transform our daily lives, our well-being, and our ability to participate in our relationships, our communities, and the world.

CHAPTER 10

Pausing in Painful Times

Doris brought her new boyfriend, Scott, to my retreat at Esalen in Big Sur, California. Scott and Doris had a crush on each other in high school. After graduation, they went their separate ways, married, and started their own families. Now both seventy-seven years old and single, they found each other again and rekindled a new zeal for life together.

Doris and Scott arrived at Esalen committed to celebrating each day together, planning to enjoy life as fully as possible.

While this was my first time meeting Scott, I had known Doris for almost ten years. Scott's affection for Doris was evident. He seemed happy to join us in the retreat and ready to jump in. Well over six feet tall with an athletic build, he looked strong and physically fit. But it wasn't until later, when we started our movement practice, that I began to notice that Scott seemed to be harboring physical pain. While he tried to hide it, his rigid movements and wincing facial expressions revealed his struggle. I later came to realize his strong exterior and perfected stoicism actually masked his daily struggle with excruciating chronic pain—for forty-nine long years.

It was a good thing Scott came to a retreat that offered a therapeutic approach and personalization of practices. However, he declined an invitation to receive individual guidance and supportive props—such as yoga blocks, a bolster, or a chair—to promote more ease and comfort during his movement. Scott was determined to get through it all by overriding his pain, something he had managed to do for a lifetime. He was driven by a motto he'd learned from his mother: "If a task is once begun, never leave it until it's done. Be the labor great or small, do it well or not at all."

Later in the session, when our larger class broke to gather in small groups for reflection and conversation, Scott slid out of class and didn't return. He also skipped the next class.

It wasn't until much later that Scott shared with me what was happening with him. "The class was so painful for me. For my body, of course, but it also brought up so much pain *about myself.* My own capabilities. The disappointment of having limitations. I wanted to be able to share this class with Doris. But there was just so much pain. I didn't want to give in to the pain. But I also didn't want to baby myself."

Scott's biggest struggle was not *actually* his pain, it was taking care of himself while he was in pain. He worked so hard to ignore it, which kept him in a cycle of struggle. He was not only caught in chronic pain, but he was also caught in chronic stress *from* his pain—and chronic stress *about* his pain.

Like most people who live with chronic pain, Scott has a story that began when he was very young. He shared, "I was the third of four boys. My parents divorced when I was very young, and my father was no longer a part of my life. My mother remarried and became extremely preoccupied, stressed, and abusive—only to be matched by my stepfather's violent temper. In those days, you just had to tough out the hard stuff. I got good at protecting myself. On top of all this, I had undiagnosed learning disabilities that made school impossible, added to my overall PTSD, and kept me in constant stress mode. But this stress also fueled my strength. I was, and still am, a tough guy. I'm tall, strong, athletic, and have worked as a contractor and a professional basketball player. I've also spent forty-seven years as an educator all over the world. I constantly pushed ahead no matter how I felt. But I've also tried *everything* to alleviate my pain. In my experience, the medical treatments just made things worse. The medications I took were often wrongly prescribed or improperly monitored, and my pain never got better. I just got better at pushing through it."

Changing Our Mind

After skipping our second class, Scott decided to come back. He missed Doris and wanted to continue his commitment to share the retreat with her.

Upon arrival, he was again offered supportive yoga props and individualized guidance to make the practice more helpful and personal. "No, thank you. I'm good," Scott said with a smile.

We began class with a formal Pause practice. We Landed, Arrived, and Relaxed on purpose. We Listened inwardly. We took a moment to check in with ourselves and Attend to whatever state we found ourselves in with curiosity and kind presence. We took another moment to set an intention to practice consciously, paying attention to our bodies, minds, and hearts to feel more grounded, open, integrated, and present.

During that Pause, Scott experienced a big shift. As he grounded, felt his breath, and relaxed more, he wondered, *Why am I pushing so hard? Why don't I adjust this practice so it's better for me?*

Then he got up and approached the assisting teachers, saying, "I would like to use the props and would take any other help you think would be good for me." Then he smiled and said, "I am allowed to change my mind."

Scott's statement may not seem like a big deal, but *changing our minds* is often something we vehemently resist—even when our stance is not necessarily serving us.

Allowing yourself to be present with how you feel and meet yourself during struggle, resistance, and pain changes the nervous system. At that moment, Scott's body got the message: *I hear you. I am here for you.*

This Listening, this *change of mind*, this compassionate response, literally changed Scott's experience of his pain. Not only did he complete the six remaining classes, but he also practiced with *ease* and in a way that helped him feel better. He allowed himself to receive the support of the teachers, but more importantly, he received his *own* loving support. At the end of one of our classes, he was so comfortable that he stayed in the rest pose even while everyone around him was rolling up their mats and gathering their belongings. "This is the first time in my life I've ever felt so relaxed," he said.

He finished the retreat feeling renewed and cared for, with a sense of connection and embodiment that cannot come from outside. This is the type of peace that can only be cultivated through meeting *yourself* with kindness, warmth, care, and compassion.

Scott returned to his daily life feeling more open, easeful, and connected, and with a completely changed perspective.

In an email to me, he wrote, "I have been suffering excruciating pain for three-quarters of my life, which has caused decades of extreme emotional and physical pain, deep sadness, stiffness, PTSD, and a debilitating shyness and self-consciousness. I'm usually not comfortable talking in groups and meeting new people. This wasn't a new insight for me, but on the second and third days of the retreat, I literally progressed from flight and freeze to freedom."

He wrote most about the compassion he was finally able to offer himself, sharing how it not only seemed to provide him more ease in his body, but also how it enabled him to connect with others in the workshop in a way that he'd never been able to before. "I also learned more about the struggles and stresses of others at the retreat and how they are working with their pain. Having more compassion for myself helped me feel more at ease and compassionate to everyone else in my group who also had their own pain. I felt like I could listen and relate in a whole new way. I felt like we were 'all in this together.' I just didn't feel so alone. Or that I had to tough it out anymore.

"The pain and stress that showed up for me were familiar and typical. What was totally new was the compassion I finally offered myself. This adjustment was a game changer. Not only did I feel better in the poses, but I also didn't leave the room when we broke into smaller groups, so I got to have conversations and connections I would normally not have experienced."

What Scott experienced is rooted in the *science of compassion*. This science shows that when we care for ourselves and treat ourselves more kindly, we can open up to others in circumstances where we would typically cut ourselves off. Even if our lack of connection with others is unintentional—even if we don't set out to go it alone—we have less capacity to connect when we are in such pain. Our pain can limit our relationships.

In changing his mind, Scott had many more moments of unexpected expansion. He shared, "When I came back and followed your guidance to 'be with what is—with no judgments and no expectations'—it gave me a new perspective and considerable relief. I learned that I didn't have to override my pain in order to feel joy."

The Story of Chronic Pain

Of course, pain is unique to each person and is also natural and essential. Pain is a critical and primary part of our survival wiring. Our first and most immediate response to the environment is to determine whether we are safe. Pain tells the body, "There is something wrong!"

It moves us to take action to protect ourselves. However, pain also activates a response that shields us from more than just immediate, acute danger.

Christiane Wolf, MD, Ph.D., and author of *Outsmart Your Pain*, is a physician turned mindfulness teacher, a senior teacher at the InsightLA meditation center, and a dear colleague and friend. Dr. Wolf notes in her teaching, "Acute pain and chronic pain are very different. Acute pain is a protective mechanism in your system; when you step on a thorn, your brain goes, *Take your foot off that thorn.* There's usually not a story. However, chronic pain tends to be overprotective. This is what I call 'the pain story.' When we're experiencing a flare-up, we're not just experiencing the pain of this moment, we're also simultaneously experiencing the memories and the trauma of the past."

I've spoken a lot about pain with Dr. Wolf, and love how she describes what is going on in the body. "Often, chronic pain involves not only 'stories' about our pain, but also feelings and expectations about our pain," she said once during a conference together. "We worry that our pain may come back or be felt in a certain way, which is also part of chronic pain. And our chronic pain may be long-standing due to the ways we've been raised or may even be inherited from those who raised us. What we do know is that acute pain helps meet an *immediate* threat, protecting us in the moment from what we need to 'survive,' whereas chronic pain can be overprotective for many of us. Keeping us protected from things in the past. It's our inner bodyguard or alarm saying, *Oh, this was dangerous before.* So then we put a lot of alarm bells around what we *think* is 'dangerous.' But there isn't always an actual correlation between the presence of tissue damage and the level of pain we're in."

When we are in chronic pain, it keeps us in a chronic stress loop. This loop keeps us from being able to choose our Response consciously.

However, as we discussed earlier, when we are under high stress, we can't just tell ourselves to relax or say, "Pain, go away." What we *can* do is learn to be with our pain—even a little bit at a time. Through titrating, we can also learn to tolerate our exposure to it, support ourselves, and send messages of care and safety during our painful experiences. This changes our experience of pain.

Meeting Pain in a New Way

Dr. Wolf also identifies self-compassion as the big game changer, saying, "Self-compassion helps to counterbalance our stress. It taps into our mammalian care system, helping us to feel soothed, connected, and more calm."

This is essential if we are going to learn to deal with pain—whatever kind of pain we may be experiencing. And there is one thing we do know about pain, whether it is physical, psychological, or emotional: It causes us to protect ourselves more.

As we practice Pausing and expanding, we begin to change our brains, allowing us to take in more than just our painful experiences. And as we open in this way, our curiosity expands, which increases our ability to *be with* what is difficult.

It's not either/or. It's never either/or. Dr. Wolf describes it instead as "Yes, and."

Aside from being a great compassion practice, "Yes, and" is also a fundamental rule of improvisational theater. In improv, "Yes, and" encourages participants to accept what another person offers (Yes) and then build upon it (and). This rule fosters creativity and ensures that the interaction continues to evolve.

Yes, there's the pain. There may also be moments of ease as well as parts of the body that may not be in pain.

This is important to remember because nothing gets our attention as pain does. Our attention collapses around our pain; it becomes the center of our world. Everything else fades, leaving us trapped in a narrow, breathless space. Pain pulls us in tight, cuts us off, and shuts us down.

This is not only true of the pain in our bodies, but it's also true of the emotional pain we feel in our hearts.

Many of us focus on the daily news—the crises occurring all over the world. This can be horrifying and stressful, and bring us to despair. But there is also beauty, love, and joy in the world. When we allow ourselves to remember this, we can open up little pockets of space.

Like Scott, many of us live with a complex inner story. "Our story" is based on what's happening now and also on our history. Many of us live with a dichotomy of feelings, simultaneously, such as suffering and joy.

We can Pause and open up our awareness, remembering that we often have various experiences at the same time. "And this too" can be here.

If there is pain in our bodies, we might say, "Yes, there's the pain here in my back, and I am also sipping this delicious cup of tea." Or "Yes, there is pain in my heart, and I also love the sound of these birds in the tree."

As we Land and feel supported, as we breathe, allow our jaw to unhinge, our shoulders to drop, and our fists to unclench, we are making space to better know and connect with our experience.

We are making space for the full range of our humanity. Rather than limiting our view and collapsing around what is painful . . . rather than assuming we have it all figured out or know what will happen . . . rather than believing it has to be this way or that way . . . we allow our experience and our lives to include all of it—the paradox and the complexity that is all true.

Maybe in that space, there is room to relate to those difficult feelings. Maybe in that space we see that this is not the *only* thing happening. Maybe there is *more* happening here. We may discover unexpected beauty alongside the pain. Maybe there is something here that is also beautiful.

As we practice not adding more tension to our experience—not causing more stress on top of what we already feel, not adding more aggression toward ourselves or the situation—we are able to widen our attention and expand our awareness into the present-moment conditions. We can see more clearly what may need our attention further.

We Are All Living in Painful Times

Dr. Wolf teaches that the part of the brain that lights up from *physical* pain is largely the same part of the brain that lights up from *emotional* pain. This means that when we break a leg, experience a stomach ulcer, tear our rotator cuff, or cut our finger while slicing a bagel, specific areas of the brain show similar activation patterns as when we are experiencing emotional pain or distress—when we feel separate, alone, hurt, or unloved. We may experience different intensities of pain, but physical and emotional pain activate overlapping areas in the brain.

She says, "Just like we have one nervous system to handle all of our real or imagined threats, we have one pain system that is triggered by actual physical injury and our ideas about what is hurtful. There is so much complexity in our pain stories right now."

What's essential to realize is that emotions like grief, sadness, loneliness, rejection, failure, or not being good enough greatly increase our experience of physical pain in general. How we talk to ourselves, our beliefs, our upbringing, and how we measure ourselves against the expectations of our culture and our social media feeds can also contribute to our pain.

Personal challenges, global conflicts, and societal divisions seem to define our world. Since how we meet ourselves will determine how we meet each other, learning to relate to our pain and offer ourselves compassion is the foundation that either opens us up to each other or closes us down to each other more. Perhaps we might ask ourselves not only how we are living with our pain, but how we are living with each other's pain.

We See Things as We Are

Anais Nin wrote, "We don't see things as they are. We see things as we are."

It is just as appropriate to say that we don't hear things as they are. Or understand things as they are. Instead, we see, hear, and understand things *as we are.*

So many of us are living in some form of chronic pain. The *pain stories* we carry will vary, but pain is pain. It's not as if one person's pain is valid and someone else's pain is not. I often hear this from students who minimize their own experience because it's not as terrible as someone else's experience. It is not a helpful practice to judge the validity of someone else's or our own pain. What matters is only that we are in pain—that they are in pain. When anyone is in pain, being met in a more supportive way—with more compassion—might help create space for them to feel more safe and, therefore, more at ease. While we know this is ultimately work we need to do for ourselves, when we do it for ourselves, it changes the way we meet others.

As we have learned, when we carry tension and are stuck in stress and pain, it's nearly impossible not to listen from a place of defensiveness. When two people meet each other at a time when both are in pain—seeking conversation or relationship or community—the interaction begins from a place of stress and self-protection. Listening curiously, openly, and deeply is physiologically *impossible* when we don't feel safe.

In my teacher training, I remind teachers that when working with "difficult" students, the student may not have a problematic *personality*. Instead, they may be in a lot of pain.

This does not apply *only* to the "difficult" people we might encounter in therapeutic environments, like meditation classes, doctors' offices, or therapists' offices. *This is us:* We are in pain—every day. We carry our pain into grocery stores, business meetings, school pickups, and family gatherings . . . at the kitchen table.

Dr. Wolf shares, "The key is rather than continually *protecting* ourselves, the way we are used to, we are kind of *retraining* the brain to calm down again. We retrain ourselves to regulate through sending messages of safety and compassion to ourselves. And to support ourselves so we can be with what is happening, rather than our story or expectation about what is happening. Of course, our pain may be hard to be with, or accept, or have compassion for. But, maybe we can start with having some compassion toward ourselves for the fact that we are in pain."

Pausing and meeting ourselves with compassion in the midst of pain can bring more ease and spaciousness to the moment we're in. Remember the snow globe metaphor? We are the sphere itself, not the snow flurries (the situations and feelings we experience). In our spaciousness, we experience much complexity, contradiction, and polarity—all swirling at the same time. Our challenge is to learn to hold space for this complexity, and incorporate it into our daily practice.

This is what Scott did. Rather than ignoring and overriding, he acknowledged not only that he felt pain, but also that he needed help. By allowing help, he felt more empowered to support himself and more able to meet his pain.

Over the six classes, Scott could relax a little bit at a time. He could deepen his breath and offer himself compassion for his story, for his pain, and for what he thought was his weakness. With this, a deeper strength emerged—the strength that comes with softly meeting our own vulnerability.

Making Space

We inherently take in the world through the filter of our habitual conditioning, which can include our anxiety, our anticipation, and our individual pain story.

Pausing doesn't eliminate pain; it creates space to experience pain without being consumed by it. This space allows us to be less reactive and more open to what is happening in the moment. It allows us to make room for our discomfort and complexity—and for the discomfort and complexity of others.

When we make space to come together without having to make things one particular way or another, we have more room to be in a relationship with each other—in whatever state we are in.

CHAPTER 11

Pausing in Our Discomfort Zone

NEUROSCIENTISTS TELL US that life changes at the end of our comfort zone. The ability to build new neural pathways is called neuroplasticity, and it happens not only from repeating "new" behaviors, but also when we reach beyond what we know and explore new territories. Whether learning a new skill or facing a fear, your brain actively creates new neural connections, enhancing cognitive abilities, memory, and overall brain health.

However, we often decide in advance how things will go, or assume we know how another person is feeling. These assumptions can keep us stuck in patterns of behaviors or relationship dynamics that simply strengthen our resistance to change. When we remind ourselves that we have space to change, we often begin to see that there might be more going on than we think. We can open up to paradox, contradiction, and complexity in ways we were not able to before.

We may realize that no way is the *only* way. That we don't need to make anything *one way*. And that things don't always have to be precisely the way we want them.

Pausing helps us create support and safety for ourselves, giving us the confidence and courage to go beyond our comfort zone. Gradually titrating, step-by-step, into new territory allows our brain to integrate these changes, leading to our personal growth and evolution.

Stuck in Our Ways

Theodor Seuss Geisel, writing under the pen name Dr. Seuss, told the story of "The Zax." There are two Zax characters, each out in the world walking on their own respective journeys. One Zax only walks north—the North-Going Zax—and the other only walks south—the South-Going-Zax. Eventually, they meet face-to-face on the north-south path, and neither will step aside to let the other go on their way.

In typical Dr. Seuss fashion, they start arguing with each other in delightful rhyme, with both the North-Going Zax and the South-Going Zax insisting that the *other* must move out of the way. They pride themselves on being dedicated to only going in their designated direction, *never* accommodating a Zax who is going in the *other* direction. They reference rules, rightness, and how they will never budge. At all. Ever.

In fact, one Zax declares quite definitively that they will never change their ways—they *never* will—even if it "makes the whole world stand still."

Despite this story being written in the 1950s, it continues to shed relevant light on how we humans tend to "meet" each other today.

Both Zax have been taught to travel on their own path without questioning if there is a better way. A different way. They've been at this for many years. They've been conditioned to move through life without considering another Zax's way or path. They don't change. They won't change.

We all learn our ways. We are socialized to *do a thing* the way we "should" do the thing.

Undoubtedly, there is room for standing firmly for what we believe in, our values, our ethics, and our vision. But if we are going to help create new ways of living together and evolving together, here . . . now, we have to be able to make room for each other. We need room to be creative and flexible—room to cooperate—to bring about change in our lives, communities, and the world.

How do we then make room for a new path together?

Limited View

Not only are we subject to conditioning from our family, culture, and peers, but we also see the world through the state of our nervous system, expectations, belief systems, and past experiences. Under the best circumstances, we have a limited view.

Even *if we could* see past our conditioning, it's rare that we slow down enough to step back and take in the *bigger picture.*

There is an ancient parable found in early Buddhist and Hindu texts about a group of blind men who learned that a fair was coming to town, bringing with it a fascinating animal called an elephant. None of them had ever encountered an elephant before and had no concept of what it might be like. Curious, they approached the animal in its pen, believing they could understand it by touching it.

The first blind man's hand landed on the trunk and said, "This creature is like a thick snake."

The next man's hand touched the elephant's ear. To him, it seemed like a kind of fan.

Another man touched its leg and said, "The elephant is a pillar, like a tree trunk."

The man who placed his hand upon the side of the elephant's body declared, "The elephant is a wall."

The one who felt its tail described it as a rope.

The last man felt its tusk and insisted the elephant was "hard and smooth, like a spear."

As each man attempted to describe the elephant based on his limited experience, their interpretations varied wildly. These differences sparked disagreements, and soon, each began to suspect the others of being dishonest.

Their arguments escalated as each insisted they were right, and eventually they erupted into a physical fight.

Our perspective is always incomplete. While our subjective experience may be valid, it is inherently limited and cannot encompass the full picture or the experiences of others. True understanding requires acknowledging that there are other truths beyond our own.

Depending on the culture telling the story, the moral of the parable varies. But it always shines a light on our tendency to claim absolute truth based on our limited experience and how we tend to ignore other people's (limited) experiences, which may be "equally true" to them.

The main teaching that has stayed with me for decades is the need for greater understanding and respect for different perspectives.

When we are under stress, our vision is further limited, impacting our ability to see a more expansive landscape, and to connect with others who view life from a different perspective. Suppose we could calm ourselves enough to open up, to listen to each other more, and expand our understanding of a situation, even if it is not familiar to us? This would set us up for collaboration or cooperation rather than conflict.

A New Path Together

Conflict and disagreement can be deeply uncomfortable, but they are not inherently *bad*. Conflict and disagreement are, and always will be, a natural part of our lives. What truly matters is how we choose to engage with and respond to them.

I remember reading a newsletter by Jeff Krasno, founder of Commune Media, the *Commune* podcast, and author of several books, including *Good Stress*. He wrote about his experience speaking at a conference a week before the 2024 US presidential election.

From the group of 250 conference attendees, he asked for two volunteers—people who were planning to vote for different candidates—to come on stage together. Dean was a white, male Donald Trump supporter, and Tara was a Persian woman who supported Kamala Harris.

Jeff began by outlining some of the key tenets of Nonviolent Communication, which was created by author and psychologist Marshall Rosenberg, that focuses on empathy, active listening, and honest self-expression. He then asked Dean and Tara to face each other for a conversation. He asked them to try to "listen to *understand*, *not* to respond," which he had described as one of the communication skills of active listening.

They were instructed to focus solely on listening, without preparing a rebuttal or even commenting on what they heard. Their task was to give their full attention to what the other person was saying. Jeff then posed three questions:

- What is your most cherished relationship?
- What was your most painful loss?
- What is your greatest dream?

Tara shared that she loves her mother, who she sadly lost last year to cancer. She also revealed that her dream was to someday be onstage at this very health and wellness conference.

Dean shared that he has three sons and that his dad had recently passed away. He dreamed of a day when grandkids would fill his home.

Jeff then guided them through a process where they repeated the other's story out loud—to each other.

They stood facing each other, staring into each other's eyes, and told each other's stories of loss, love, and hope. Their eyes filled with tears; it was clear that both Dean and Tara felt seen and heard.

Jeff then asked Tara and Dean to offer four or five reasons why they were supporting their respective candidates. The instructions were the same as before: Just listen. No commenting or responding.

Tara felt passionate about having a female leader. Dean valued his First Amendment freedoms.

Jeff then asked them to repeat what they heard, emphasizing what was important to the other person without simplifying or diminishing the other person.

Still staring at Tara, Dean reiterated her argument about the importance of female leadership (and actually agreed with it). Tara, in turn, echoed Dean's regard for free speech.

As the conversation closed, the audience applauded as these courageous humans hugged each other.

Jeff closed his story by sharing that, in the end, neither Dean nor Tara changed their minds. There was no attacking each other. Neither was vilified or victimized. They *both* felt seen and not judged. They recognized the *humanity* in each other.

For a brief moment, neither person was a symbol of their political affiliation, but rather "just a person"—with important relationships, profound love, loss, and dreams.

Currently, we live in a country that has become polarized in many ways—ideologically, culturally, politically. In such a polarized world, it's easy to develop the conviction that the "other side" is wrong and must change. But if we are going to create change together, we first need mutual care, mutual respect, and understanding. It is only by recognizing the humanity in *all of us* that we can cooperate and collaborate—and ultimately, change.

As Jeff also noted in his newsletter, our hard conversations are not confined to the politics of the moment. There are many difficult conversations that we might need to have on a daily basis. If Dean and Tara can stand on the stage and engage, maybe we, too, can summon the courage for those hard discussions with our families, friends, and neighbors.

The questions I've been asking myself more and more are these: Can we de-escalate conflict enough to foster connection rather than deepen division? Instead of entrenching ourselves in the roles of "us versus them," can we transform our conflicts into opportunities for growth and evolution?

Curiosity: The Cornerstone of Connection

Dr. Gail Parker, psychologist, international presenter, and author of the self-care book *Restorative Yoga for Ethnic and Race-Based Stress and Trauma*, emphasizes that curiosity is essential for opening space in our conversations for connection.

Dr. Parker and I have taught several workshops together, during which she explains intricacies of creating connection, particularly among disparate groups of people. She says, "You can make someone else feel safe when you are curious rather than judgmental, assuming, or indifferent. In the face of listening to others, especially those we don't know so well or those from another culture, it's important to remember that we can't know everything about others or every culture, but what we can do is be curious about others."

As I've discussed throughout this book, Listening includes being aware of ourselves and how we feel while conversing with another. In this way, we can learn to notice our own expectations and emotions, stay curious about ourselves, and hold space for ourselves and the other person.

Dr. Parker suggests Pausing to check in with ourselves during conversations, with questions like:

- Am I truly listening?
- Am I making assumptions?
- Do I have expectations?
- What am I feeling?

If we can stay aware of ourselves and curious about our feelings, we won't get *stuck* in what we are feeling. "A key to remember is that if we can *notice* when we are in the stress response, we are not stuck in it," she says.

Hala Khouri, author of several books, co-editor of *Practicing Liberation: Transformative Strategies for Collective Healing and Systems Change*, and co-founder of the social activism organization Off the Mat, Into the World, also emphasizes curiosity as an essential cornerstone for connection in difficult conversations.

Khouri, who is also a therapist, yoga teacher, and somatic experience practitioner, contends that curiosity is not only a portal for going deeper into our conversations, but is also the key to helping us know when it is time to *leave* a conversation—or not have one at all.

In an interview I hosted, she said, "When we are in conversation with another, I think it is important to ask ourselves, *can I be curious right now?* If we *can't* get curious, that might be a good indicator that we need a break or need to remove ourselves from the conversation or situation, if that is an option."

Again, the main point is that we need to stay connected to ourselves so we can sense our internal state. True listening *requires* curiosity. If we can't be curious, that's essential information for us. And, when we are highly activated in the stress response, we cannot simultaneously be curious. That part of our brain is not accessible when we are in fight-or-flight mode.

Whenever you notice you can't be curious, take a moment to Pause—maybe go to another room, go outside, slip off to the bathroom. Anywhere. Pause and care for yourself until you can get your curiosity back.

You May Be Wrong, But You May Be Right

If we could consciously choose to enter conversations with the intention to Listen—to be curious—to understand the other person's experience a little bit better, maybe even put ourselves in their shoes, we might be able to learn from people in our lives whose worldviews are different from ours or even opposed to ours.

It can be helpful to remember that leading with curiosity *rather than certainty* doesn't automatically mean that someone else is right. Or that we are wrong. But it opens a space in which we might connect rather than shut down to each other. The goal is not necessarily to reach agreement with others, but to understand each other. For many, this is a radical idea.

Dr. Parker emphasizes that harmonious relationships require awareness, not agreement. In fact, insisting on an agreement can be a hostile act. She says that the search for *agreement* can often lead to arguments because it invalidates the other person's perspective, whereas the search for *understanding* dissolves the barriers that result in discord and harm and allows us to get to know one another.

In one of our many Zoom talks, she explained it like this: "If I need to be right, then I'm *not* going to be able to listen to you *unless* you are in agreement with me. *And*, if I need to be right, it means either you have to agree with me or you're wrong. The need to be right means that somebody else has to be wrong. Who likes to be wrong? Nobody. Nobody wants to be made to feel like they're wrong. Making someone wrong will most likely push them into a protective stance. But, when we approach someone with curiosity, it creates a whole new opening to make a connection with each other.

We might say to them, 'Tell me more . . . I'm really interested in that . . . I never thought about it that way.'"

When we are in difficult or uncomfortable conversations, can we create space to listen to each other with our differences? Can we create space for communication and connection for its *own* sake rather than for someone to be right and another to be wrong? How can we learn to understand each other rather than agree? How can we treat each other (and ourselves) better *while* learning to better understand each other and our different perspectives?

Pausing with the intention to prioritize *Listening before speaking* helps us regulate our nervous system so that we can not only create this space, but we are also less likely to activate someone else's stress response. During our interview, Khouri said, "Imagine two nervous systems on high alert trying to have a conversation, it's almost impossible! Especially if both parties are vying for being right. If you want to disrupt that pattern, you need to figure out how to self-regulate; part of that is about tolerating the discomfort of disagreeing with someone or being in conflict."

She continued, "One of the most interesting things I've discovered in my work, is that when people feel really, really listened to, they themselves are more willing to try to understand the other person, even when they don't agree. Through this type of listening, I've seen some people with very strong convictions and beliefs loosen their grip on their own fixed ideas and start to open up their perspective or get greater understanding and empathy for a different perspective."

If we can Pause during a contentious situation and shift into curiosity, we might stay in the conversation long enough to ask questions that help us get to know someone, and listen in a way that makes them feel genuinely heard.

When people feel heard and acknowledged, they are more likely to feel safe enough to listen in return. If we want to be heard and understood, it often starts with ensuring that the other person feels heard *first*. This of course takes practice.

Across the Divide

We often enter conversations intending to prove our point or convince someone of something. We don't make space to see, hear, or learn from the person in front of us. All effort is invested in reinforcing our point of view. How can we avoid resorting to more polarizing positions?

In an interview with David Remnick in *The New Yorker* magazine and podcast, Sarah Elizabeth McBride, a Delaware senator and author of *Tomorrow Will Be Different*, shared her ideas about how change happens among groups with divisive viewpoints, specifically regarding human rights policies.

Senator McBride emphasized the importance of helping people feel "okay" with being on opposing sides of an issue—that just because someone is on "the other side" of an issue does not make them a *bad* person.

McBride said, "I think one of the reasons why we see people pushed into their respective corners is because you say something that's *deemed* problematic, and you are immediately hounded by one side and immediately embraced by the other side. Human nature is to—when faced with that degree of extreme binary reactions—go to the people who are validating you instantaneously. We unintentionally actually push people further and further into their own corners and into their negative opinion by responding with a degree of condemnation and vitriol that creates no incentive and space for them to grow . . . I think all of us need to do a better job of seeing the humanity of people on the other side of the aisle. Because I think what happens in this country right now is: The left says to the right, 'What do you know about pain, white straight man? My pain is real, as an L.G.B.T.Q. person.' And the right says to the left, 'What do you know about pain, college-educated, cosmopolitan élite? My pain is real, in a post-industrial community ravaged by the opioid crisis.' And I know that, when I am upset, the worst thing that someone can say to me, even if it is said with the best of intentions, is 'It's not as bad as you think.' Any therapist will tell you that the first step to healing is to have your pain seen and validated."

This is true not only in the realm of civil rights or during political discourse. We see this in our everyday lives all the time—parents who disagree on child-rearing strategies, such as how or when to discipline—or health beliefs like to vax or not to vax. We all have different beliefs about things and we often go to the mat for them, even within our closest relationships. This does not usually foster a sense of connection.

Feeling Heard, Feeling Felt

Feeling felt is a term coined by Dr. Dan Siegel. It is used to describe a sense of being understood and a sense of connection. During a 2011 conference at the Garrison Institute, in Garrison, New York, Dr. Siegel said, "Wonderful things happen when people feel felt—when they sense that their minds are held within another's mind."

Feeling felt is yet another way our nervous system experiences safety.

Remember in Chapter 3, I talked about how, when we bring our attention to what is underneath us, we allow ourselves to feel supported, which sends a message to the brain that we are safe. Sensing support is key to someone feeling safe. Similarly, I discussed that when we Listen to someone in a way that leaves them feeling heard, it lights up the part of their brain that leaves them feeling loved. When we offer someone our empathy, it leaves them feeling felt, creating a sense of connection between us. We not only feel safe with the other person, but we also feel a sense of safety in the connection—which enables us to further receive empathy and have empathy for others.

Empathy is essential for connection and collaboration.

We are neurologically wired to connect. Science has shown that we have a type of brain cell that "mirrors" what we perceive from others; these brain cells are called mirror neurons. When we observe someone feeling an emotion, our mirror neurons light up. To our brain, it's as if we *ourselves* are experiencing the emotion.

Mirror neurons are linked to our ability to be empathetic, helping us to put ourselves in another person's shoes. When we see someone feeling sad, our mirror neurons fire, allowing us also to experience sadness—to feel empathy. We don't need to "think" about the other person being sad; we can experience the emotion ourselves.

When we practice LAR-LAR and notice how we feel, we may get further information about what is happening with those around us.

We are *always* communicating with those around us. Whether through our words, movement, behavior, or the subtle expressions on our faces, we constantly communicate how we feel—even when we are not trying to.

As we perceive another person, we can practice Pausing and tuning in to ourselves to better sense what is happening in the moment. If we can sense that the other person is angry, we can take a breath to Pause, to check in. Pausing allows us to shift into curiosity mode, helping us to consider what may be going on beneath the surface.

What might the person really be feeling? Are they frustrated? Are they anxious? Do they feel hurt? Maybe they're in pain—physical or emotional. Perhaps they are going through a personal crisis. Perhaps they are juggling a million balls. Perhaps they just didn't sleep well last night—or for the last week—or for years.

Part of what we can take away from Scott's pain story in Chapter 10 is how to approach not only our *own* pain, but also the pain of *others*. There may be "Scotts" around us all the time—in front of us in line at the grocery store, driving in the next lane on the highway, or sitting next to us at the kitchen table—people who may truly benefit from being met with empathy and understanding.

As we Pause, as we grow grounded in our own bodies, as we become present and relaxed, we can be more curious. We can be more steady and rooted, even while someone else is not—even when someone else is confrontational, even if someone else needs to be right, even when someone is in pain. When we can be more regulated ourselves, that other person may be able to feel more safe and eventually calm themselves as well.

This is important when we are connecting with others and in conversation with others. Especially in hard conversations.

Creating Space for Discomfort . . . and Change

If we want to change how we react to a situation, *we need to be in the situation and have a new experience of it.* We need to be able to say to ourselves, *I'm going to do this new thing, or do my old thing in a new way—and I'm going to do it* with *all of my old discomfort.*

While it's beneficial to learn to Pause in challenging or uncomfortable situations, it's equally important to know when it is not wise to Pause. It's obviously not the time to Pause when you need to swerve out of the path of an oncoming car. Similarly, in times of high anxiety, and particularly trauma, Pausing may be too overwhelming, agitating, and even exacerbate your state.

For times like these, there are additional techniques and steps to support you in adapting the LAR-LAR practice. These instructions are included in Chapter 15.

However, in most cases, expanding our capacity to step into situations, conversations, or relationships where we need to put aside our expectations can be a great growth opportunity. When we begin with an attitude of openness to the "unknown," we can grow our capacity to better handle ambiguity, change, paradox, and uncertainty.

I don't know about you, but tolerating someone else's pain, specifically my child's, has been one of the hardest things for me to practice. As a mother, my knee-jerk response is wanting to make things better. To change and fix and solve the hard feelings Willow has to go through. Or any of my loved ones, for that matter.

I remember being in the car with Willow after one of her earliest heartbreaks. She initially reacted with anger, her voice crescendoing into a stream of choice words. I, too, tensed up, holding my breath, my shoulders hiked up to my ears, and my fingers gripping the steering wheel alongside my suffering daughter. I wanted to tell her how she *could* respond. How she *should* feel. How all of this would eventually pass. But I also knew that, despite my good intentions, this would probably lead to angry words between *us*. So, before words came out of my mouth, I Paused.

I took a breath to drop my shoulders and loosen my grip on the wheel. I took another breath to acknowledge the pain—both hers *and mine.*

I just Paused and breathed, and in that space, Willow began to shift from raging to crying. Messy crying. It was then that my heart really dropped. Her anger was easier for me to tolerate than her sadness; hearing her express her heart pain was brutal.

I took a breath. I reached out and put my hand reassuringly over her hand. Over the next few minutes—minutes that seemed like an eternity—she shifted from a hard messy cry to a soft weep. Each time I felt myself wanting to say something, I took a breath and dropped my shoulders again. And again. And again.

Then, for a second time, things unfolded in an unusual way; this time, for Willow. After her rage, after her messy cry, and then her soft weep, she caught her own breath. Exhausted, she took a big exhale and just sat quietly for the rest of the ride. As we pulled up to home, Willow said, "I really needed to let myself cry. Thank you."

This was a first for both of us. A first for me to stay out of the way while staying fully present. And a first for her, to have the space to go through her full range of feelings. I was grounded and open enough to feel myself *feeling* Willow's experience without trying to *change it.* And this left her *feeling felt.*

Willow's disappointment did not disappear. She was still hurt and sad. But she was also more relaxed and at ease. We both were. We were each in a more spacious state, and while we didn't necessarily feel happier, we both felt more connected and intimate with each other. We both felt the love between us.

CHAPTER 12

Pausing Is an Act of Love

One of my favorite poems to share during teaching is "The Question" by Rosemerry Wahtola Trommer:

> All day, I replay these words. Is this the path of love?
> I think of them as I rise, as I wake my children,
> as I wash dishes, as I drive too close behind the slow
> blue Subaru.
> *Is this the path of love?*
> Think of these words as I stand in the grocery store.
> Think of them as I sit on the couch with my daughter.
> Amazing how quickly six words become a compass.
> The new lens through which to see myself in the world.
> I notice what the question is not.
> Not, "Is this right?" Not, "Is this wrong?"
> It just longs to know how the action of existence links us to the
> path of love.

And is it *this*? Is it *this*?
All day, I let myself be led by the question.
And all day, I let myself not be too certain.
Is this the path of love? Is it *this*? *Is this the path of love?*
I ask as I wait for the next word to come.

Is this the path of love is the main question I ask daily, too. It is the North Star of my Pausing practice. Does what I'm doing now leave me feeling more connected or separate? Am I opening up or closing down? Is this the path of love? Or am I strengthening the impulse for division or feelings of fear?

I Pause and ask over and over again: Is this the path of love?

It's an open-ended question, an inquiry. I do not have the answer. There is no fixed answer. The answer is a moment-to-moment decision, a choice we make. A choice you make.

It's a practice in which we wake up every day and choose again. Choose. Choose.

When our nervous system is stuck in stress mode, everything feels like a threat, leaving us with limited choices. So the guiding questions are: How do we lean toward love and connection? How do we not add aggression to the moment? It all starts with regulating the nervous system.

We Pause. We ask. And we must not be too sure of the answer. We allow ourselves to be guided in each moment as we Attend to ourselves as best as we can.

In a conversation with Krista Tippett, on her *On Being* podcast, former United States Surgeon General Vivek Murthy, author of *Together*, beautifully said, "What can we do in our lives through the decisions we make, the choices we make, to tip the scales in the world away from fear and toward love?"

Like most people, I often struggle with fear. Now, instead of getting upset that I'm fearful, I try to remember to put my hand on my heart and remind myself that, in this moment, it makes sense that I would feel afraid, confused, or uncertain.

This awareness is what choosing love looks like.

Making the effort to try and remember to Pause is an act of love to myself. Forgiving myself when I have forgotten to do so is also an act of love. Each time I try to soothe and comfort myself, it is an act of love. All of these acts of love change the nervous system.

It doesn't mean I'm not going to have fear—or anger or rage or grief. I had a combination of all these things when I left my mom and my daughter at the table.

When we recognize feelings of fear, rage, or grief, and forgive ourselves for the ones we think are "bad," we offer ourselves compassion, leaving us feeling more open and grounded. It leaves us more able to follow the path of love.

The Brutiful

Life is both awful and awesome, wretched and glorious, brutal and beautiful. It always contains contradictions and polarities. It's never either/or.

However, while both the brutal and the beautiful exist, we are predisposed to notice the awful, wretched, and brutal more. Remember the negativity bias I discussed in Chapter 7? Dr. Rick Hanson describes it this way: "The brain is like Velcro for negative experiences and Teflon for positive ones."

This tendency is amplified and strengthened further when we are stressed, conditioning our implicit memory—the memory that holds our underlying beliefs and patterning below our conscious awareness—leaving us focused even more on the negative.

Not only do we tend to focus on the brutal, but we also inadvertently strengthen that tendency when we try so hard to change, fix, control, or avoid our discomfort or challenges altogether. Even though it may sound contradictory, this resistance to the brutal only further limits our experience of the beautiful, which is also present in our lives.

Glennon Doyle, author and host of the *We Can Do Hard Things* podcast, writes in her book *Carry On, Warrior: Thoughts on Life Unarmed*, "Life is brutal. And, it's also beautiful. Life is Brutiful."

Suffering is indeed an unavoidable fact of human experience. The suffering on the planet is more and more palpable. Global illnesses and wars make our future feel uncertain. Amid all this chaos and collective stress, we may feel unable to see what is also beautiful in our lives. But suffering is not the whole story; it's not the entire truth.

As Zen Master and Vietnamese Buddhist Monk Thich Nhat Hanh famously taught, "Life is filled with suffering, but it is also filled with many wonders, like the blue sky, the sunshine, the eyes of a baby. To suffer is not enough. We must also be in touch with the wonders of life. Wherever we are, any time, we have the capacity to enjoy the sunshine, the presence of each other, the sensation of our breathing . . ."

Still, most of us need to consciously Pause to see beyond our suffering and take in life's wonders on purpose. This doesn't mean these things of beauty are not right there in front of us. It simply means when we are stressed, and our negativity bias is dominant, we are not able to notice what is also there.

Doyle reminds us, "Life's brutal and beautiful are woven together so tightly that they can't be separated. Reject the brutal, reject the beauty." If we are going to tune in to the sunshine and the wonders of life and enjoy them more readily, we will need to make some extra effort—and we will need to train in doing so.

We practice on purpose with little things. Not with our enemies, not with the people who berate us, not with our difficult bosses or our most challenging conditions. We don't start there.

We start with simple things that irritate us just enough that we can practice Pausing in front of them and not flipping our lids. When we are behind that too-slow Subaru, or that person in the grocery store with thirty items to check out in the ten-and-under line, can we Pause, breathe, and relax on purpose? Can we calm ourselves so we don't grow reactive, or have tunnel vision, over what we are irritated, aggravated, or annoyed by? Can we Pause, ground, open, and take in more of the present moment? Can we notice anything beautiful that may also be in front of us?

This practice progressively increases our ability to work with more difficult circumstances and challenging environments. It allows us to be open to all that is going on, expanding our ability to choose how we Respond.

The Brutal

We all go through it all, the wretched and the glorious.

For most of us, being with difficult feelings and experiences is among the most complex challenges in our lives. But being with others' difficult feelings, with someone else's pain, can be just as hard—sometimes even harder. We have an instinct to make things better. Even things like loss or other things we can't change, we want to somehow resolve something.

Sitting with someone else's pain challenges our natural inclination to want to fix or save others when they are struggling, instead requiring us to simply be present, listen deeply, and allow them space and time to process their own experience without imposing our perspective or solutions on them.

The more we are able to be with our own discomfort and pain, the more able we are to acknowledge and be with others' experiences. After all, pain and suffering are a normal part of the human experience. The more intimate we are with understanding how our pain makes us feel, think, and behave, the easier it is for us to understand others. Our suffering is a portal to understanding and connectedness with ourselves, others, and all of humanity.

Author Leo Buscaglia illustrates this connectedness with a story about a four-year-old boy whose next-door neighbor was an elderly gentleman. The man's wife had recently died, and one day, when the little boy saw the man crying, he went into the man's yard, climbed onto his lap, and sat there.

Later, the boy's mother asked him what he had said to their neighbor. "Nothing," he replied. "I just helped him cry."

All humans experience pain and suffering; despite how different it can be for each of us, it is a deeply shared experience, especially grief and loss. We all will lose someone or something we love. Our lives will painfully change at one time or another. We all have to go through difficult feelings where we don't know when or if we will get to the other side. When we Pause and Listen, allowing ourselves to acknowledge and truly feel our own pain, we become better equipped to relate to others—even those we don't know well or may not even favor. This sense of connectedness empowers us to make wiser, more compassionate choices for one another.

We Pause and Attend to ourselves as our first act of love—so that we can attend to others from a place of love.

Just Like Me

While often urging us to appreciate the beauty of life, Thich Nhat Hanh never taught us to ignore what is happening. His primary teaching is that love is understanding, and if we want to love others and ourselves, we must listen to and understand one another's suffering.

There is a Buddhist meditation called metta meditation. It is an ancient practice that helps us cultivate compassion for ourselves and others. One modern technique is to use it in our daily lives. As we walk through the world, we Pause and see others—on the street, in the dog park, at the conference table, on the train, or in the slow Subaru. As we look at these people (even for a brief moment), we say in our heads, *Just like me.*

Maybe we say:

Just like me, this person knows suffering.

Just like me, this person knows pain.

Just like me, this person wants to be happy and at ease.

Just like me, this person wants to feel loved.

As we do this, we see ourselves in others and feel our interconnectedness. We are all part of the human condition. *Just like me, they suffer, are in pain, make mistakes, and experience sadness.* No one escapes suffering. Every single person has struggles and challenges.

The more we can give ourselves compassion, the more we can give compassion to others.

The Beautiful

There may be days when seeing the good is an effort. Sometimes, it might be hard to give others grace. Sometimes we can get stuck wondering if they deserve it or not. And sometimes it's just neurologically impossible to focus on anything positive.

Remember, we are not trying to override or deny how we feel or what we are experiencing. Instead, we are Pausing to expand our attention, which will help create conditions for expanding our minds, lives, and Responses in the present moment.

Dr. Hanson writes in his blog that when you notice good moments on purpose, "they'll collect in implicit memory, deep down in your brain. In the famous saying, 'neurons that fire together, wire together,' the more you get your neurons firing about positive facts, the more they'll be wiring up positive neural structures."

Dr. Hanson calls this practice "Taking in the Good." It involves consciously noting positive experiences—not only beauty, but also feelings of gratitude. This includes recognizing a good quality in yourself, or acknowledging something you have done well—and savoring the experience for ten to thirty seconds to let your brain and body soak it up. He writes, "Taking in the Good sculpts your brain. It's like building a muscle."

We've all heard the aphorism "Stop and smell the roses." As a teenager, I would be so irritated when my mother suggested this cliched idea, but I have grown to know what good advice it is. Research shows that emotional states like appreciation, gratitude, awe, and reverence positively impact physical, psychological, and even spiritual well-being. Studies have shown that consciously entering these states more often will lead to increased health and happiness overall, as well as a stronger connection to others, nature, and life itself.

Pausing to notice beauty re-wires our brains to see and enjoy it more often.

Practicing joy may seem difficult, trite, or even offensive in a world on fire. Some people may even feel guilty when they catch themselves being joyful.

But we also know that our emotional responses to a barrage of bad news or bad experiences can create a constant state of stress, take a serious toll on our health, and significantly inhibit our ability to show up when others and the world need us most. Stress can greatly diminish our capacity to connect with each other.

Eventually, this re-wiring helps us keep our minds more open. It enhances our ability to be present, curious, and compassionate. Allowing ourselves to connect with sources of beauty and joy brings us both spaciousness and well-being, as well as resources and renewed energy. It gives us a feeling of connection to something greater, a sense of belonging, and gratitude.

Expanding our awareness each day to include Taking in the Good strengthens our capacity to navigate and hold our suffering. Focusing solely on suffering, however, diminishes our resilience and well-being—both physically and mentally—and restricts our ability to respond effectively to life as it unfolds.

When we Pause, we create the conditions to remain open to the brutiful—the brutal and beautiful—that lives within us and around us. This openness allows us to truly observe and experience life while expanding our capacity to choose how to respond to what unfolds.

Even with all the strife and challenges in our lives, this helps us to be more warm toward each other rather than reinforcing our impulse to close down or separate.

Again, practicing noting beauty, joy, gratitude, or ease doesn't mean you have to be falsely positive. Instead, it is about having tools and techniques to meet ourselves, our emotions, and the present moment and each other with care.

I have repeatedly experienced that the more I practice taking in the good, noticing beauty, and feeling gratitude, the more it happens organically, even when I least expect it and when it is most needed.

I was recently working with my editor to try to meet the deadlines for this book. Having just returned from leading a weeklong retreat, and balancing my time with caring for an ill loved one, I was exhausted and stressed about the work ahead of me. Our session was interrupted by an urgent call from my veterinarian. To say my stomach dropped is an understatement. My beloved pup, Sunday, now twelve years old, had just had a biopsy. While not a certified therapy dog per se, there is no doubt Sunday is our therapy dog, *my* therapy dog, and has been our family's source of comfort through many brutiful times.

The strangest thing happened as I stepped outside to return the doctor's call. I was struck by the stunning autumn foliage of our Japanese maple tree—and simlutanesously shocked to experience this effortless sense of awe just as I was about to make a phone call I feared so deeply. Not only did I notice the tree's inspiring beauty, but it also interrupted my panic.

This nature *intervention* slowed me down. I was able to calm myself, which completely changed how I got on the phone.

Upon hello, the vet affirmed that Sunday had a very fast-spreading cancer. Though devastated and heartbroken, I was still present, able to listen and ask all the essential questions.

My open state did not make the vet's news less significant or less difficult. Instead, it gave me more capacity to accept it and stay in the conversation instead of slipping into panic mode, which would have been so natural for me in a moment like this. This allowed me to respond better in a more effective and needed way.

Had I not received the blessing of beauty from the maple tree, I would not have had as many resources for myself, nor would I have been able to be a source of calm for my family. This ability to witness opposing "truths" at the same time isn't only possible and normal, it can also be medicinal.

To Be With

Seeking rest and renewal, Dusty, a first-time student, attended my Esalen retreat, The Sacred Pause, a few months after having major surgery. On the final morning of the retreat, he had a transformative experience.

During a run along the Big Sur coastline, Dusty was struck by the beauty of the crashing waves, the crisp air, and the lush succulents surrounding him. In that moment of awe, he felt the strong presence of his mother, who had passed away a year earlier.

Grounded and present, Dusty found himself able to *be with* her memory in a new way. Thoughts about his beloved mother, which were once unbearably painful, now became fully accessible to him. They expanded into something wonderful and healing.

The ability to connect more intimately with ourselves and our lives not only requires a decision to be open to what is, but also requires caring for ourselves so we can make space for these sacred experiences.

Dusty later reflected that while he came to the retreat to recover from surgery, what he truly needed was space to grieve. That realization, born in a moment of connection with nature and his own emotions, stayed with him long after the retreat. After he went home, he continued his practice of Pausing to be present with all his feelings, the easy and the difficult . . . the tragic and the tender. The brutal and the beautiful.

Pause to Smell the Roses

Most of us need to make a little extra effort to Pause and Take in the Good—to feel safe enough to "slow down and smell the roses"—to notice and even allow ourselves the positive experiences that are a breath away.

Wired to survive, our inherent tendency to process negative information over positive information is an unconscious, immediate, and dominant brain state. In other words, negative experiences overpower positive ones. Dr. Hanson writes that a single bad event (like the bad review about my workshop) is more memorable than ten thousand good ones. But we can learn to pay attention to the good things in our world to level the playing field. We can learn to remember the whole story.

Pausing in nature doesn't just give us a break—it actively supports our well-being, both mentally and physically. When we take a moment to be present outdoors, we can reduce stress, ease anxiety, and even improve focus and mood. These moments of connection with the natural world also enhance our empathy, cooperation, and sense of belonging, making us feel more connected to ourselves and others.

By combining Pausing with time in nature—whether through a mindful walk, breathing in fresh air, or simply noticing a tree swaying in the wind—we create space for our nervous systems to reset. This practice not only helps us feel grounded in the moment, but also builds resilience and fosters a deeper appreciation for the world around us.

What's even more fascinating is that whether it is a stroll through a city park, hiking in the wilderness, or even imagining natural environments you have previously spent time in, people have been shown to reap similar health benefits. Even looking at a photograph of nature can offer these same benefits.

Research also shows that Pausing can be easier with nature's help. During my Instagram Live interview with Micah Mortali, author of *Rewilding* and founder of the School of Mindful Outdoor Leadership at the Kripalu Center for Yoga & Health, he explained how our nervous systems respond to natural settings, saying that mindful states of awareness are more a part of normal life when we are immersed in our natural habitat, the outdoors. He also noted that Pausing may be more effortless outside.

He said, "In my experience, and that of many of my students, it is generally easier to Pause—to be mindful—in nature compared to other environments, as the calming and sensory-rich qualities of natural surroundings can help to organically focus our attention on the present moment and promote a sense of ease, relaxation, and well-being."

Spending more time walking with awareness outdoors, conscious of our breathing, and curious about what we can perceive through our senses, we can enjoy more of the beauty and fascination that is all around us.

Coming Home to Our True Nature

I have been profoundly influenced by the philosophy, "We are not in nature, we are nature," which I learned through my studies in

Ayurveda, an ancient Indian system of medicine and the sister science of yoga.

A favorite quote that I often use in my workshops is from Andy Goldsworthy, an environmentalist and outdoor sculpture artist: "When we say that we have lost our connection to nature, we are saying we've lost our connection to ourselves." Reconnecting with nature is not just about stepping outside—it's about rediscovering our own rhythms and belonging. As poet and priest John O'Donohue writes, "Our bodies know that they belong; it is our minds that make our lives so homeless."

To bridge this disconnection, we can start with simple practices: spending time outdoors, attuning to natural rhythms like sunrise and sunset, and even pausing to breathe deeply and notice the world around us. These small, mindful actions help us feel more grounded in ourselves and more connected to others.

Pausing in nature is a powerful way to remember our interconnectedness. When we come home to our bodies on the earth, even for a breath or two, and tune in for just a few moments, we can turn our awareness back outward in a new way.

Each time we Pause and find a deeper connection with our hearts, each time we come home to listen to ourselves, we have more resources to meet each other and the world around us with empathy, compassion, kindness, and love.

Survival of the Kindest

Today's research confirms that having the capacity to collaborate and bond with others—to feel care, warmth, and sympathy—is at the heart of what helps our species survive. Malcolm X said, "When 'I' is replaced by 'we,' even illness becomes wellness."

Dr. Laurie Santos, host of the *Happiness Lab* podcast, produced an episode that discussed how cooperation, kindness, and compassion in the animal kingdom and the human world prove to be at the heart of our ability to thrive.

Dr. Santos and her guests discussed that the most popular understanding of Charles Darwin's concept of "survival of the fittest" is that those who have physical and mental prowess, who dominate others, will be most likely to survive. However, contrary to this point of view, some scientists have contended that Darwin's work suggests something closer to "survival of the kindest" or "survival of the most cooperative" as more accurately explaining which species adapt and thrive—that cooperation has been more important than competition in evolutionary success.

The podcast team went on to discuss the work of Russian scientist Peter Kropotkin, who in 1842 studied how animals in Siberia, Russia, survive in the harshest conditions in the world, amid continual blizzards and temperatures of minus sixty degrees. Rather than animals competing, Kropotkin discovered that the ones that survived were those that cooperated. He found evidence of this everywhere.

The team talked extensively about how animals and insects collaborate to build homes and hives, hunt, and gather for protection. One example was a story about a species of solitary beetle that buried food underground to feed their larvae—if the food was big, like a dead mouse or a bird, sometimes ten other beetles would arrive to lend a hand.

Kropotkin concluded that there was competition, but not against each other. Instead, the competition was against a harsh natural world. He observed this not only in animals, but also in Russian peasants who helped one another thrive in harsh conditions.

The key to survival was helping each other overcome the difficulties of living through challenges.

As we Pause to remember our connectedness, we expand our capacity to Respond with cooperation and collaboration. This is good not only for us individually, but also for us as a whole.

At a recent retreat, Grace, a student in the group, shared, "Last night you talked about how we were all in the same boat. And it made me think . . . If we are literally all in the same boat, I don't want the boat to sink."

Her words struck a chord. It's not that we're in one boat and those we disagree with are in another boat. When we truly embrace this understanding, no one wants the boat to sink. The question then becomes: How do we work together to keep it afloat—for all of us?

We Need Each Other

We don't know what is truly happening inside another person, and we don't know what others are carrying into our conversations or when we meet. What we do know is that we need each other.

We need each other.

Spiritual teacher and author Ram Dass taught, "Essentially, the only thing you can truly offer another person is your own state of being . . ."

Pausing gives us the tools to regulate our nervous system and choose how we show up in our moments. To a large extent, this state of being is the one thing we can control.

We can practice deliberately, with intention, all day long—for a lifetime. There is no finish line. Pausing is a choice we must make repeatedly, over and over again. It may not make for a catchy social media post, but that's the reality of how it's done.

In the beginning, I'd set the alarm on my phone at least three times a day. Or pick an activity I did a couple of times a day and let that be the reminder to practice. I often practice the first LAR before meals, taking three breaths to Pause before I eat. I practice during conversations with my adoring daughter—who, on occasion, drives me a little crazy. I take three breaths to relax and open, especially in those moments when I feel the impulse to do the opposite.

Just because we're practicing doesn't mean the impulse to do the opposite goes away. We're practicing relaxing with the impulse to do the opposite.

When I'm feeling irritable, I remind myself that I'm practicing. I might still say something I regret, but I'll take responsibility and apologize more quickly. I'll explain what I was feeling and acknowledge that it wasn't the other person's responsibility.

I'll be the first to admit—this takes practice.

It also takes courage. The courage to be vulnerable. The courage to sit with that vulnerability.

Above all, it takes courage to choose the path of love.

Each Pause is an act of love—a choice to meet life and each other with greater care.

CHAPTER 13

Coming Home to the Sacred Present

For years, I've taught the Pause practice LAR-LAR as a way to come home to the present moment. It wasn't until one of my Portuguese students, Eugenia, shared that "lar" means "home" in her language that I realized how perfectly this aligned with the practice. This magical coincidence deepened my understanding of what it means to come home—to a place of refuge, care, and connection.

I delved deeper and discovered that in Portuguese, *casa* translates to "house," while *lar* conveys the deeper, more personal essence of "home." Unlike a mere physical dwelling, "lar" signifies an emotional connection and a reverence for the space we call home. This distinction is beautifully captured in the phrase "home sweet home," which becomes *lar doce lar* in Portuguese.

Interestingly, "lar" would *also* be the preferred word choice for an institution for people or animals needing care or aid—another remarkable parallel for our Pause practice. In the Pause, there is a refuge, a welcoming space, and the infinite new now. Our true home, the present moment, is always here for us.

If our true home is the sacred present moment, Pausing is the doorway.

Pausing is the foundation of mindfulness, offering us a way to slow down and fully arrive in the present moment—the space where life is happening. Author Joseph Campbell suggests that what we truly seek is not the meaning of life, but the experience of being fully alive—a connection between our physical experiences and our inner reality, where we can feel the rapture of life itself.

We long to be here, *now*—where life *is* happening. It is the *only* place where life is happening. We long to feel alive and in a relationship, in partnership, with life. Yet, who among us has not had the experience of being somewhere special and sacred—the birth of a child, our own wedding, a reunion with a loved one—and later realized we can't remember much of what happened? We were there, but we were not truly present.

Imagine if we knew how to pause to savor a moment of ease, joy, celebration, and sacredness—to be present and experience the quality and connection of what was happening right in front of us. Imagine if we could genuinely savor the rich, meaningful moments of our lives—not just the "big" milestones, but also the small joys and the quiet beauty surrounding us each day.

We long for it and put so much pressure on ourselves to experience it, yet we keep missing out on our lives. So often, we focus on analyzing what is happening instead of fully experiencing it. We put so much pressure on ourselves to do everything right. To be a good parent, partner, child, friend, employee, boss, maker, creator, meditator, or whatever the label may be. As we work so hard at life, we miss out on experiencing what is truly important to us, on *experiencing* our lives.

If the first LAR is the Pause that brings us home, the second LAR is how we can inhabit our home. We embody ourselves to be with the present. By practicing the second LAR, we allow ourselves to inhabit *home* truly. We learn to bring our presence into the Present moment to experience the aliveness and sacredness of the ever-new now.

When we Pause and come home into the present, we make space to feel more intimate and enriched by life as it happens. Of course, we will also encounter our most challenging moments, but we will also experience the fullness of life—aliveness. LAR-LAR helps us come home to experience the wholeness and holiness of life itself.

Pausing reminds us of what truly matters: Life is important, we are important, and this moment is worth experiencing. It is worth choosing how we want to meet it—how we wish to participate and respond. Pausing creates the conditions in our body and mind to make that choice. And, as Viktor Frankl said, "In our response, lies our growth and our freedom."

The Future Is Here

Can we let go of the idea that everything must be solved or perfect before we allow ourselves to be fully present and alive?

Artist Mary Engelbreit has written: "Don't ever save anything for a special occasion. Being alive is the special occasion."

Even in the brutality of our world and lives, there is beauty—here and now, in the sacred moment.

When we Pause and reorient ourselves to the present, we not only experience the aliveness of this moment, but also how we engage with it. How we meet this moment shapes our ability to meet the next one—and every moment that follows. Consciously choosing how we wish to participate, respond, and collaborate with the moment unfolding before us shapes not only our future but also the future of our world.

Coming back here, now, is where this all happens. And we do it over and over again.

There's no singular, magical moment when we're done.

Pausing and coming back home—into our bodies, into the present—is a daily practice, a moment-to-moment choice, and a way of life. Some days, it feels effortless; other days, nearly impossible. But we always have the choice to return, Pause, and be here—again and again.

This is the most powerful teaching I have ever received: We don't have to wait for New Year's, our birthday, a holiday, the start of the week, or even the following day to begin again. We can choose to Pause—right here, right now—and decide how we wish to participate in this moment.

We are practicing Pausing to Land, Arrive, Relax, Listen, and Attend so that we can Respond—choose how we want to be with this one precious life—this one precious moment—and experience being alive in the world with each other.

May we Pause to welcome ourselves back again and again. In doing so, may we create a more loving present and compassionate future for all.

CHAPTER 14

May We Remember

LET'S TAKE A moment to Pause together. Here, now.

May you begin by sending a message to yourself that you are welcome here, just as you are now.

May you allow your body weight to rest fully on the earth.

May you allow yourself to Land in the spot where you are, just as you are. Here, now.

May you allow your breath to Arrive in your body.

May you allow your mind to Arrive on the flow of the breath as it moves through you.

May you Arrive home in your body, with your breath, into the present moment. Here, now.

Even if only for one breath.

May you allow yourself to Relax—*whatever* you can relax.

May you release your excessive holding:

May you unclench, may you soften, may you unfurl.

May you let your body relax here, now, on the ground, in the spot where you are.

Even if only for one breath,

May you allow yourself to Land, Arrive, Relax, and feel your belongingness—in your body on *our* earth.

May you feel your breath, our breath—the one ocean of air surrounding—feeding—and enlivening all of us—connecting you to all of creation.

May you know your interconnectedness.

May you relax, expanding into the spaciousness that is always here for you.

Spaciousness that is here, now.

May you Pause. And in this space, may you Listen.

May you Listen inwardly to your body, heart, and mind.

May you Listen outwardly to the world around you, to those around you.

May you Listen to what is here—without trying to solve or change.

Simply Listen to what is, just as it is.

May you remember to Pause: to Land, Arrive, and Relax

So you have the space to Listen and Attend.

So you have the support you need to be with life as it's happening, just as it is, just as you are.

May you Pause to Listen and Attend to yourself and whatever you carry with kindness, curiosity, and compassion.

May you be easy with yourself and your feelings of restlessness.

May you *be with* your restlessness, too.

May you forgive yourself for your urges to fix, bury, ignore, judge, berate, shame.

May you hold your own heart, your body, your mind, and your life in friendship.

May you Attend to yourself through it all, knowing you are cared for.

May you Land, Arrive, and Relax; may you Listen and Attend so that you may meet yourself with the care and support you need to choose how you wish to Respond, behave, act, and be in this present moment.

May you remember that each and every time you Pause, you have more choices for how to Respond, engage with, contribute to, participate in, and collaborate with the present moment. With each other.

May you remember that your response ripples out to affect everyone you come into contact with.

May we remember that Pausing *is* an act of love.

Pausing is an act of love.

And may we remember that each time we Pause, we can contribute to a more just, peaceful, and loving world. One breath, one moment, one choice at a time.

PART THREE

PRACTICING

This section is divided into two chapters. Chapter 15 provides guidance, somatic tools, and techniques; these can be helpful for all of us, but are of great service for those practicing with excessive bodily tension, higher levels of anxiety, and the challenging conditions of trauma. Chapter 16 introduces additional practices that can deepen your experience with various aspects of LAR-LAR and Pausing.

To enhance your experience, all the practices in *The Power of the Pause* are available as audio recordings. You can access them for free at https://jillianpransky.com/powerofthepause-practices or with the QR code on page xii.

CHAPTER 15

Practicing with Excess Tension or When Navigating Anxiety, Trauma, or PTSD

The somatic practices and tools I offer here may benefit anyone at any time, helping to release excess stress and tension, discharge pent-up energy, and unblock stuck emotions in the body. In fact, most of us will benefit from a few moments of bodily movement as a helpful transition into Pausing. However, the tools in this chapter are an essential support for those working with higher levels of anxiety or navigating trauma.

These techniques can be used in two ways within your Pause practice. First, they can serve as preparatory steps to help ground you before engaging in the stages of LAR-LAR. For example, practices like bouncing, tapping, or humming can help bring the nervous system into a more regulated state, making it easier to transition into Landing, Arriving, and Relaxing.

Alternatively, these techniques can be integrated directly into LAR-LAR itself. For example, during the Landing phase, you might incorporate a gentle bounce to connect with your body while feeling the ground beneath you. In fact, you might even continue bouncing during the entire LAR-LAR practice. This adaptation allows the practice to meet you where you are, tailoring it to your unique needs in each moment. You are encouraged to continually adapt the practice to fit your nervous system, body, and mind in a way that is personal to you.

Please remember, LAR-LAR does not have to be done in stillness, ever. Landing can be practiced while walking or running, as we feel our feet contact the ground. Your Pause practice can be as dynamic or as still as feels right for you. If you wish to explore the LAR-LAR practice in more stillness, allow this to be a gradual progression over time. Bit by bit—breath by breath.

Lastly, LAR-LAR is not recommended during a panic attack, flashbacks, or acute danger. Also, if you are aware that you are dealing with anxiety, trauma, or PTSD, I highly suggest working with professional support along with these practices.

General Guidance for Techniques for Anxiety, Trauma, or PTSD

Choose a somatic technique from pages 226–230 that resonates with you and try it for one to ten minutes (or whatever duration feels right for you). You can use it before the LAR-LAR Pause practice or following an initial Landing practice. After completing one of the techniques, you can return to the Landing step and gradually add the following two steps: Arrive and Relax.

For some, tuning in to how we feel—internally and externally—can be overwhelming at first and therefore it may feel best to skip the Listening stage of LAR-LAR, or do so with the support of a therapist.

Instead, you can go directly from Landing, Arriving, and Relaxing to Attending, offering yourself a gesture of presence, support, and compassion. Whenever you are ready, you can incorporate the Listening step into your practice.

General Base LAR-LAR Guidance (Insert Technique of Choice)

Here is some guidance for the overall practice, with a space holder where you would insert your choice of technique:

- Notice where your body meets support. Imagine the earth underneath this support, there to hold you.
- **Land:** Take the next three exhales, perhaps out of your mouth. If you wish, add an audible sigh. Let your body weight Land entirely on the ground. Notice how the ground, or whatever is under you, supports you fully.
- **Add your technique of choice from pages 226–230.**
- **Land Again:** On the next three exhales, sense yourself Landing on the ground.
- **Arrive:** For the next three breaths, you may wish to place your hands on your belly or place one hand on your belly and one hand on your chest.
- Bring your awareness to the feeling of the breath moving under your hands. Let your mind rest with the feeling of the breath under your hands.
- As your breath arrives in your body, let your mind Arrive on the breath.
- **Relax:** For the next three exhales, release three habitual areas of tension, such as your jaw, shoulders, and fists.

- Please Pause here for a moment. Consider concluding the practice. You can also go straight to Attend.
- **Attend:** Place your hand on your heart or anywhere on your body. Offer yourself a gesture of presence, support, and compassion.
- Pause here to close the practice. Set an intention to return to Pause throughout the day.
- As you become more conscious of your regulation *over time*, you may wish to add the step of **Listening** to your practice (check in with your doctor about this). When you are ready, take a few gentle breaths of Listening to check in with yourself. Ask with a soft curiosity: *How am I right now, in this very moment? Here, now?*

CHOOSE YOUR TECHNIQUE

You can do one or any combination of these techniques at any time. By incorporating these techniques into your Pause practice, you can gently guide yourself toward greater calm and self-awareness, and support yourself even during moments of heightened anxiety or trauma.

Bounce/Shake: An Energy Balancing Technique

This technique helps release pent-up energy and tension through movement. On the flip side, it can also be used when feeling lethargic and needing to lift your energy a bit. While this is most often practiced standing, you can also practice it seated by bouncing/shaking in your seat. Allow your body to bounce gently, starting with your knees and progressing to your torso and arms. Keep your movements loose and fluid for one to ten minutes.

1. If you are standing, have your feet at least shoulder distance apart and knees slightly bent.
2. Relax your jaw, let your head rest on your neck, and let your shoulders rest on your body. Relax your arms, elbows, and hands.
3. Begin gently bouncing your whole body (without letting your feet leave the ground). The knees bend to generate this bouncing action. If you are seated, this is more of a shake.
4. Let your bounce come from the bottom up. Start by allowing the ripple to come up your legs and spread the movement to your torso, chest, shoulders, and arms. Allow your whole body to become loose while you bounce and/or shake. You can continue this for one to ten minutes.
5. When you feel complete, slow down the bounce to gradually approach stillness. However, you might prefer to continue a subtle bounce throughout the next few steps. You don't need to be still for them.

Squeeze and Release: A Progressive Relaxation Technique

This technique deepens our relaxation by gently physically squeezing and releasing our muscles, relieving excess tension and inviting us to open up space for a little more calm. You are welcome to do this seated, lying down, or standing.

1. Begin by finding a comfortable position. Rest your arms by your sides.

2. Take three deep breaths inhaling through your nose and exhaling from your mouth. Gently stretch your breath a little longer than natural. Allow your jaw to release open as you exhale. Continue breathing like this as we add a squeeze and release, beginning with the upper body.
3. As you inhale, gently make a fist to tense the muscles from your knuckles to your shoulders. Shrug your shoulders up. As you exhale, release your upper body completely. One more time, inhaling, the whole upper body firms, and exhaling, the entire upper body softens.
4. Move your awareness to your lower body. As you inhale, slowly squeeze your seat, firm your thighs, and scrunch your toes. Let your seat, thighs, and feet completely release as you exhale. Allow your weight to drain down onto the ground. Repeat the lower body one more time. On your inhale, squeeze your entire lower body. On your exhale, relax your lower body completely.
5. This time, squeeze your whole body equally everywhere. As you inhale, squeeze everything in and up. As you exhale, release everywhere, entirely. Repeat this one more time. Pause and allow your weight to drain down onto the ground. Let your whole body be at ease, even for just one breath. Jaw dangles; arms and shoulders drape down; hands unfurl; seat, legs, and feet are at ease.
6. You can do this again as many times as you wish. When you feel complete, move into Landing.

Hum or Voo Vocalization: Techniques to Stimulate the Vagus Nerve

Humming is a yogic tool that has long been used to calm the nervous system. Humming creates vibrations that stimulate the vagus nerve (the switch that helps turn on the parasympathetic nervous system), which runs through the larynx and pharynx in your throat to help us balance our fight-flight response.

Trauma expert and author Peter Levine uses a specific kind of vocalization, the Voo Breath, in his trauma-informed system of Somatic Experiencing. This breath is proven to have an effect on the same systems as humming does and has been shown to directly activate the vagus nerve.

One difference between these two techniques is that you hum while breathing in and out through your nose, your lips gently touching. However, making the sound of voo (like a foghorn) requires exhaling out of your mouth.

1. To begin, sit comfortably, as upright and as relaxed as possible.
2. Take one full breath in and out before you start vocalizing on the next breath.

Choose Hum or Voo (or Any Combination of the Two)

To Hum: Inhale deeply through your nose, then exhale slowly out your nose while you make a humming sound, your lips gently resting on each other. You may feel the sound vibrating through your mouth, head, and body. Pause for a natural breath or two. Repeat.

To Voo: Inhale deeply through your nose, then as you exhale slowly through your mouth, make a resounding "voo" sound. You might feel the sound resonating throughout your chest and body. Pause for a natural breath or two. Repeat. You can enjoy several Voo Breaths, ensuring that you pause for a natural breath or two between the breaths.

"I Am, Here Now" Affirmation: A Technique to Help Grow Focused and Present

When our minds are overactive, it can be very beneficial to give our minds an activity to engage in—which can help us create a focal point and anchor our attention. Using an affirmation (mantra) can be very helpful in engaging the mind while also helping to center in the here and now.

1. Pause and sense where your body meets the ground.
2. Bring your hands together in a prayer-like position.
3. Press your palms together on your inhale and extend your hands toward the sky.
4. On your exhale, slide your prayer hands gently back to your heart.
5. Now add the mantra: On your inhale, raise your hands to the sky *and* mentally chant, "*I am.*" On your exhale, bring your hands back to your heart and mentally chant, "*Here now.*"
6. On your inhale, *I am*. On your exhale, *here now.*
7. Repeat these breaths with the movement and mantra for as long as it is helpful.

CHAPTER 16

Extended Mindfulness Practices to Enhance Your Pause Practice

THE MINDFULNESS PRACTICES in this chapter will help enhance your experience and skillfulness with LAR-LAR and Pausing and offer you further training in calming your nervous system and expanding your awareness. *These practices can be integrated either before or after LAR-LAR. For audio recordings of these practices,* *see the QR code on page xii.*

If You Need More Landing: Mindful Walking

Mindful walking is a simple and effective tool for grounding yourself. As a daily practice, mindful walking can significantly impact your day and your life.

Mindful walking was born out of traditional walking meditation, an ancient practice that has its roots in Zen Buddhism. It is a meditation in action. It has evolved as a modern mindfulness practice made popular by Thich Nhat Hanh.

What I love about mindful walking is that it helps us learn how to bring the Pause into our daily lives rather than having to stop an activity to practice. In fact, mindful walking can actually be done anytime while walking.

Try it when you leave your house—on your way to your car or the train, getting the mail or taking out the garbage, walking the dog, or even just up and down the steps of your house or building. You can do it every day, any time. Experiment with longer mindful walks in a park, the woods, or even around town.

You can begin or end your Mindful Walking practice with LAR-LAR.

Begin by Pausing to ground yourself. Stand tall with your feet hip-width apart and notice the sensation of your feet connecting to the ground. On a long exhale, allow yourself to Land more. Let your shoulders fall away from your ears and allow your weight to settle closer to the ground. Allow your feet to spread in your shoes, as if filling out their outline.

Start walking at a pace that feels naturally slow and comfortable. There's no need to move very slowly—just enough to become fully aware of the sensation of your feet connecting with the ground and the rhythm of your breath moving in and out of your body.

Gently focus on your pace and feet as you expand your awareness into the world around you—the sights, sounds, smells, and activity in your environment (traffic, nature, etc.). Just notice what is around you, without fixating on anything; simply let everything flow past you as you move.

As you walk, notice the sensations of your feet on the ground, the movement of your body, and continue to spread your awareness to include the sights, sounds, and smells around you—taking in as much as feels comfortable.

When your mind drifts or becomes distracted by your thoughts—or something other than your walk—don't make a big deal about it. Gently draw yourself back to the present by refocusing on how your feet feel meeting the ground. Notice the sensations in your heels, then your toes. Eventually, bring your awareness to sense your whole body walking. Then, once again, take in the world around you. It doesn't matter how many times you become distracted while walking. The benefit of the practice is in the act of noticing that you are distracted and choosing to come back. Returning your attention again and again to sensing your feet. Returning to presence.

To close, return to sense your feet connecting to the ground. Feel your breath flowing through your body. Re-relax. Let your shoulders fall away from your ears and allow your weight to settle closer to the ground. Let yourself Land completely. Set an intention to return to walking mindfully throughout your day, even if only for a few steps.

If You Need More Relaxation and Openness: Sky Gazing

I learned this meditation from Pema Chödrön. It's straightforward and always available. While it is basically a Pause to gaze out into the expansive sky, it works to create a sense of spaciousness within you at many levels. It is a simple and relaxing technique.

In short, the sky gazing practice comes from the Dzogchen Buddhism tradition, which is considered to have originated in Tibet between the seventh and ninth centuries CE. Dzogchen teaches that our essential nature is always free from limitations and emphasizes the practice of resting our minds in a natural state free from conceptual thinking, which is sometimes described as our "primordial state." This natural state (like the Pause itself) is said to be wide open and clear. Like the open sky, the weather may flow through; clouds come, and clouds go. But the infinite sky remains open. As Pema Chödrön is quoted as saying, "You are the sky; everything else is the weather."

Since the sky is always there and will always be there, we can gaze at it like a teacher, reminding us how to open. Gazing at the sky also helps our minds feel less narrow and constricted and more relaxed. Even if there is no sky from our vantage point or it is cloudy, we can imagine a sky or look at a photograph of a sky.

Find a place with a good view of the sky. If possible, position yourself where you can take in an expansive view of the sky. You can be at a window or outside. If a view is not available, choose a photograph, or use your imagination.

Find a comfortable position seated, standing, or lying down. (You can also lie on your back outside.)

Land: On the next exhale, perhaps out of your mouth, add an audible sigh. Let your body weight Land entirely on the ground. Notice how the ground or whatever is under you supports you fully.

Arrive: Let your mind rest with the feeling of the breath as it flows through your body. As your breath arrives in your body, let your mind Arrive on the breath.

Relax: On your next exhale, release three habitual areas of tension, such as your jaw, shoulders, and hands.

Gaze out into the sky. Notice the expansive space of the infinite sky. Although clouds may move through it, the sky stays wide open.

To expand your awareness, as you gaze out into the spaciousness of the sky, also sense your breath flowing through you. Imagine your breath softening you inside, gently expanding the space inside your body. Your body and mind growing more relaxed and open.

Imagine the same infinite space that endlessly expands outwardly also expanding inward without limit. Imagine your mind as vast and open as the sky. Imagine your heart taking the shape of the sky. We are deeply interconnected within this continuum of space.

To close, return to feel the support underneath you. Sense your body grounded, your breath flowing freely, your mind present and open. Set an intention to remember the image of the sky throughout your day as needed.

Enhance Belonging and Interconnectedness with Our Infinite Breath

Breathing meditations can further connect you to the flow of life and the shared experience of breath. Life begins with the breath, so our relationship with air is fundamental to everything else. However, there is also much more to the act of breathing and the exchange of air than just receiving oxygen and releasing carbon dioxide.

As we breathe, we are participating in a global exchange—a reminder that every breath connects us to the living world and to each other. The breath is not just a metaphor; it is the invisible web that connects us to one another and everything around us, both seen and unseen, fostering a more profound sense of belonging.

David Suzuki writes, "Every breath is a sacrament, an affirmation of our connection with all other living things, a renewal of our link with our ancestors and a contribution to generations yet to come. Our breath is a part of life's breath, the ocean of air that envelops the earth."

While practicing, we might imagine the continuum of the infinite breath. We can place our awareness on the breath constantly moving through us—in and out—at every moment. This visualizing can be another way of opening while remembering our interconnectedness.

Paying attention to the breath can connect us to our *true home* in the infinite new now while also bringing us back into our own human body. The air we breathe connects us to our own embodied experience and to others as we all breathe into this global atmosphere, shared resource, and ultimately collective energy.

Classic Breathing Meditation Practice

Take a moment to allow yourself to Land on the ground. Let the ground hold you. Let your attention gently slide toward the area where you most feel your breath's presence.

You may wish to place your hands on your body and feel your breath moving under them. Maybe you feel movement in your belly or chest. You may feel your shoulders rise or the skin on your chest stretch. Perhaps you simply feel sensations of temperature in your nostrils. See if you can *feel* just one full breath as it moves through you, from the beginning to the middle to the end.

See if you can mentally trace just one complete breath. Follow your breath with your awareness from beginning to middle to end. Allow your mind to rest on the flow of the breath while you follow the air as it moves from the space around you into your body. Then, follow the air as it moves back out.

Imagine the one ocean of air that surrounds all of creation also flows through you. One ocean of air, waves of breath flowing through everyone.

Imagine your inhale was someone else's exhale and your exhale will be someone else's inhale. Simply rest your mind on *our* breath as it flows through you.

When you notice that your attention has pulled away from your breath, you can gently guide your awareness back to your breath. When you notice thoughts, images, emotions, or sensations arise, just let them flow on by. You don't have to dialogue, comment, or respond to them. You don't have to ignore them, stop them, push them away, or follow after them. When you notice sound in the room, you don't have to zoom in or try to shut it out.

It doesn't matter how many times your attention leaves your breath. You simply welcome yourself back, shepherding yourself back to the breath again. This is the practice: noticing when you are not with the breath and caringly drawing yourself back over and over again. Allow yourself to be aware of your breathing. To forget and to return.

Now, shift your attention to your heart area. You might place one hand over the center of your chest to feel your breath expanding under your hand. Imagine you could breathe directly through your heart as if you had nostrils on your chest, where the breath moved in and out.

As your breath comes in, imagine it gently expanding your heart space. Allow the breath, our breath, to softly expand your heart center, caressing and easing any rigidity it comes into contact with. Allow our breath, the one ocean of air, to gently, caringly flow through you.

Allow your mind to Arrive on the breath, affirming your connectedness to all things.

The breath is always welcoming you. You are welcome here now. Just as you are. Welcome yourself, just as you are, into this moment, just as it is.

When you feel complete, you may Pause to close the practice with LAR-LAR.

ACKNOWLEDGMENTS

With profound gratitude, I acknowledge the many people whose support, guidance, and generosity made this work possible.

I have been blessed to study with some of the greatest meditation and yoga masters of our time, each of whom has profoundly shaped my path. I am most especially grateful to Pema Chödrön. My life truly transformed when I began integrating her teachings, and I am forever humbled and inspired by her humanity, mastery, generosity, and compassion.

With deep reverence, I thank Erich Schiffmann, whose influence on my practice and life is immeasurable. I am also tremendously grateful to Dr. Ruella Frank for helping me to integrate somatic awareness and experiencing into my life. My studies with Jack Kornfield, Tara Brach, Ram Dass, and Sharon Salzberg have deeply enriched my practice of compassion, presence, and openness—for which I am endlessly appreciative.

As a yoga therapist and teacher trainer, I continually study the work of healers, doctors, and neurologists to integrate the most up-to-date research in mind-body medicine. I am especially grateful for the contributions of Drs. Herbert Benson, Daniel Siegel, Richard Davidson, and Rick Hanson.

I also extend my gratitude to my colleagues and friends—expert guest teachers in my Restorative Training Program—whose insights continue to deepen my practice and life: Dr. Gail Parker, Dr. Christiane Wolf, Hala Khouri, Lisa Weinert, Tracee Stanley, and Indu Arora.

I bow to my students from nearly thirty years of classes and trainings, who are a constant source of inspiration, insight, and friendship. My deepest thanks to my retreat communities—Kripalu, Omega, Esalen, Blue Spirit, and Feathered Pipe.

I am immensely grateful for my online studio community—the sangha that has held and sustained me and my work since March 2020. Every gathering, from Friday meditations to membership classes and trainings, has filled my heart, strengthened my resilience, and fueled my passion to share this work. Though scattered across the world, we remain forever connected through the heart of the practice.

So many people work behind the scenes to support me—managing events, promoting programs, and ensuring my work reaches those who need it. Some have been with me for years, and I extend a heartfelt thank you to Rasmani Deborah Orth, Patti McCabe, and the production teams at Kripalu, Omega (Brett Bevell, Gillian Arthur), Esalen (Frederica Helmiere, Camille Wright, Cara Chandler), Blue Spirit (Stephan Rechtshaffen), and Feathered Pipe (Eric Myers, Crystal Water). And a heartfelt bow to my dear friends and musical collaborators, the amazing Garth Stevenson, Kristen Ambrosi, and Scott E. Moore.

Words cannot fully express my gratitude for my personal management and support team. I simply could not have continued my work through COVID and for the past six years without the magnificent Deanna Michalopoulos. She has been the driving force behind my transition online and wears many hats in my organization. Her diligence, wisdom, humor, and compassion have been an essential cornerstone in my work and personal journey. I am also blessed with the support of Jamie Brotz, who manages the many ways I communicate digitally. Her loving friendship and enthusiasm for the practice continually nourish my work and life exponentially. And to Kristen Sparro, who wholeheartedly assists me and the whole community in a variety of ways. Her presence, friendship, and laughter have been a divine gift in my life.

Deep gratitude to my SiSTARS—Andrea Silk, Deanna Michalopoulos, Gina Vecchitto, Jamie Brotz, Jennifer Kurdyla, Kristen Sparro, Kristen Ambrosi, Larissa Noto, Lisa Jardine, Nicole Ruffo, and Susannah Owen. Their love and support have lifted my heart and spirit in ways I can never fully express.

Deep thanks to Katherine Zimmermann, my editor at Union Square & Co. (Hachette), for her passion for *The Power of the Pause* from the very beginning and for championing my work. Gratefulness to Barbara Berger, also my editor, who guided and shepherded *The Power of the Pause* into the world. And to publisher Emily Meehan, editorial director Amanda Englander, and the incredible team at Union Square: project editor Kristin Mandaglio, copy editor Lynn Northrup, interior designer Christine Heun, cover designer Patrick Sullivan, creative director Lisa Forde, production manager Anais Villa Gray—your support has meant everything.

To my agent, Ellen Scordato at Stonesong—thank you for lighting the fire to get this book out into the world and for finding it the perfect home.

Endless gratitude to Lisa Weinert for encouraging me and helping me launch my proposal. To Elizabeth Keenan, editor extraordinaire, who brought clarity, polish, expert guidance, and unwavering enthusiasm to this project. And to copy editors Linda Federico-O'Murchu and Jennifer Kurdyla for their invaluable final reads.

I could not have written this book without my partner in crime, Jessica Wolf. She walked beside me every step (and every word) of the way—her mentorship, wisdom, and masterful writing not only helped shape this book but have enriched my life for nearly thirty years. The year I spent writing *The Power of the Pause* was one of the hardest of my life (a story for another time . . . perhaps another book), and Jessica held my hand and helped me through every moment (and every page of this book). A simple thank-you will never be enough.

To my family—I am so grateful for your love and support. Thank you always, Mom and Dad (Phyllis and Paul); Scott, Judy, and Danielle; Bennett, Kelly, and Easton; Nicole; Bob and Anne; Norma; Jodi, Doug, Zach, and Josh. An extra pause for Jodi and Scott Bienenfeld—the dearest of friends, who were an indispensable lifeline during my year of writing.

And with all my heart, my deepest gratitude to my husband, Brad, and daughter, Willow—for your unwavering belief in me and for your patience and support throughout this journey. Your love is my foundation. Thank you—you are my people.

And to you, dear reader—thank you for meeting me here and for practicing Pausing.

When we Pause, the benefits extend beyond ourselves. It ripples into our relationships, our communities, and the world at large. In this way, Pausing is a fundamental and powerful act of peace. Thank you for being part of this practice—and for helping to make the world a better place.

ABOUT THE AUTHOR

Monika Broz

Jillian Pransky has taught mindfulness, yoga, and meditation internationally for over thirty years—helping people feel at home in their bodies and meet the present moment with greater clarity, choice, and compassion. Known for bridging the gap between body and mind, she creates immersive experiences for seasoned yoga and meditation teachers as well as first-time skeptics—especially those seeking relief from anxiety, pain, or trauma. Jillian teaches at many renowned holistic learning centers, including Kripalu, Omega, Esalen, and Mohonk Mountain House. Her acclaimed book, *Deep Listening: A Healing Practice to Calm Your Body, Clear Your Mind, and Open Your Heart*, is now in its third printing. She lives in New Jersey with her family and their beloved Muppet-like dog, Sunday.